THE WAY
OF THE BELLY

Also by Neena & Veena

DVDs and Videos

Ancient Essentials
Bellydance Core Conditioning
Bellydance Fitness for Beginners: Arms & Abs
Bellydance Fitness for Beginners: Basic Moves
Bellydance Fitness for Beginners: Fat Burning
Bellydance Fitness for Beginners: Hips, Buns, & Thighs
Bellydance Fitness for Beginners: Slim Down
Discover Bellydance: Basic Dance
Discover Bellydance: Beyond Basic Dance
Discover Bellydance: Mystic Dance
Indi-Hop

Also by Nancy Bruning

Books

Dare to Lose: 4 Simple Steps to a Better Body
(with Shari Lieberman, Ph.D.)

Effortless Beauty: 10 Steps to Inner and Outer Radiance the Ayurvedic Way
(with Dr. Helen M. Thomas)

The Real Vitamin & Mineral Book
(with Shari Lieberman, Ph.D.)

Rhythms and Cycles: Sacred Patterns in Everyday Life

Swimming for Total Fitness
(with Jane Katz, Ed.D.)

✳ ✳ ✳

Please visit Hay House USA: **www.hayhouse.com**
Hay House Australia: **www.hayhouse.com.au**
Hay House UK: **www.hayhouse.co.uk**
Hay House South Africa: **orders@psdprom.co.za**

THE WAY OF THE BELLY

8 ESSENTIAL SECRETS OF BEAUTY, SENSUALITY, HEALTH, HAPPINESS, AND OUTRAGEOUS FUN

Neena & Veena

WITH NANCY BRUNING

HAY HOUSE, INC.
Carlsbad, California
London • Sydney • Johannesburg
Vancouver • Hong Kong

Published and distributed in the United States by: Hay House, Inc., P.O. Box 5100, Carlsbad, CA 92018-5100 • *Phone:* (760) 431-7695 or (800) 654-5126 • *Fax:* (760) 431-6948 or (800) 650-5115 • www.hayhouse.com • ***Published and distributed in Australia by:*** Hay House Australia Pty. Ltd., 18/36 Ralph St., Alexandria NSW 2015 • *Phone:* 612-9669-4299 • *Fax:* 612-9669-4144 • www.hayhouse.com.au • ***Published and distributed in the United Kingdom by:*** Hay House UK, Ltd. • Unit 62, Canalot Studios • 222 Kensal Rd., London W10 5BN • *Phone:* 44-20-8962-1230 • *Fax:* 44-20-8962-1239 • www.hayhouse.co.uk • ***Published and distributed in the Republic of South Africa by:*** Hay House SA (Pty), Ltd., P.O. Box 990, Witkoppen 2068 • *Phone/Fax:* 27-11-706-6612 • orders@psdprom.co.za • ***Distributed in Canada by:*** Raincoast • 9050 Shaughnessy St., Vancouver, B.C. V6P 6E5 • *Phone:* (604) 323-7100 • *Fax:* (604) 323-2600

Editorial supervision: Jill Kramer   *Design:* Amy Gingery
All photos by Ed Freeman, except those on pages 104 and 172, which are by Michael Higgins.

Library of Congress Cataloging-in-Publication Data

Neena.
  The way of the belly : 8 essential secrets of beauty, sensuality, health, happiness, and outrageous fun / Neena & Veena with Nancy Bruning.
    p. cm.
  ISBN-13: 978-1-4019-0613-9 (hardcover)
  ISBN-10: 1-4019-0613-3 (hardcover)
  ISBN-13: 978-1-4019-0615-3 (tradepaper)
  ISBN-10: 1-4019-0615-X (tradepaper)
 1. Belly dance. 2. Belly dance--Health aspects. 3. Beauty, Personal. 4. Body, Human--Symbolic aspects. I. Veena (Veena Bidasha) II. Bruning, Nancy. III. Title.
  GV1798.5.N44 2006
  793.3--dc22   2005017172

09 08 07 06   4 3 2 1
1st printing, February 2006

Printed in China by Imago

A very special thanks to our heavenly and spiritual Mother and Father Gods, for their love and support

CONTENTS

PREFACE

by Neena & Veena

Our unique destiny made itself known early in our lives. We have always loved to dance, sing, and act; and even as young as five years old, we put on a never-ending array of our own little made-up musicals and plays for our family. It didn't matter that all we had was a makeshift stage set off by an old sheet draped over a rope as a curtain that stretched across the main room of our family's ramshackle farmhouse. The magic was there, and performing was already in our blood when we caught our first glimpse of a belly dancer at a family function.

We were mesmerized by her colorful costume, her exotic movements, and the music she danced to. She delivered everything our young hearts yearned for: captivating looks, an aura of mystery, an element of the risqué, and the total embodiment of supple yet strong femininity. That moment of color, sound, and motion sealed our fate. Belly dance had spoken to us—and we were hooked!

Fast-forward several years: We were 14 years old and were at long last attending our first belly-dance class. Not having a clue about what to wear, we both showed up in T-shirts, while the other students wore short tops that exposed their midriffs. We couldn't help but notice bellies of all shapes and sizes: small, big, tight, jiggly, or poochy. But once the music started, these women shimmied, swirled, and shook—they just totally let themselves go.

Wow! What an eye opener! Never before had we felt such an explosion of uninhibited female energy, of women who were proud of who they were—including their bellies. Every cell in our young bodies said, "Yes! Yes! Yes!" In spite of our ignorance, we knew that something special was happening in that class, and we were transformed. We knew—right then and there—that belly dance had to be a big part of our lives.

From that day on, we immersed our bodies, minds, and souls in the dazzling sensations of our chosen life. Today, thanks to the power of that world—the epitome of sensuality, femininity, and sexuality—we've become known as the Bellytwins.

The road wasn't always easy, and we've faced many challenges along the way, including the disapproval of becoming belly dancers from our parents and other family members. But it sure has been worth it. We've accomplished all of this by knowing, deep down in our bellies, what was right for us. By being ourselves, we're fulfilling our unique destiny.

Now just as we found a way to create our own path to a joyful life, we want to help you do the same. No matter who you are—whether a bank executive, librarian, homemaker, graphic designer, or florist—*The Way of the Belly* will show you the fun, sensual, feminine way to become the person you want to be!

✳ ✳ ✳ ✳ ✳ ✳

Introduction

Living the Good Life, with a Twist . . .
and a Shimmy, a Hip Circle, and a Great Big Smile!
by Neena & Veena

Whose life couldn't use an extra dose of sensuality, beauty, rhythm, lightness, playfulness, and fun? Let's face it: There's not one woman out there who doesn't crave at least a little bit of attention. Whether we're thin, heavy, short, tall, young, old, blonde, or brunette, we all desire to be beautiful. And guess what? We already are! Women are perfect beings because we all come with unique gifts, yet we always strive to look prettier, sexier, and younger, and to feel more energetic.

As profesional dancers, both of us need to look good and feel great whether we're in front of a camera or onstage in front of a live audience. But when you think about it, whether you're out running errands or out on the town, all women have an audience, and that's men! And yet even women observe other women, which means the entire public is your stage. So, we all want to look and feel our best—that is, our poise, confidence, taking care of ourselves, and making the most of what we've got. Women are always asking us how we do it—looking and feeling good while keeping up with this insane pace of shows and appearances.

So we'd like to introduce you to *The Way of the Belly,* a unique lifestyle that makes women look and feel exotic, attractive, and more—a program that blends our Eastern culture with Western ideas. In these pages, we'll share secrets for controlling our weight and toning our bodies, having clear skin and shiny hair, eating healthy foods, listening and tuning in to ourselves, and maintaining our cool under stress—all without losing our sense of humor, keeping a positive outlook while being true to ourselves.

We'll show you how to transform your look the Bellytwins way so that you can be your own "belly queen" with bold colors and style through makeup, clothing, jewelry, and lots of fun and sexy sparkles! We're not saying that every woman needs to become a belly dancer. By "transform," we simply mean opening your world to changes and allowing yourself to become more of who you really are, and not trying to meet someone else's standard of beauty, style, or achievement.

In this book, you'll learn how to enhance your gifts and individuality and accentuate the positive, no matter what your cultural background is. As a woman, you're a creative, active creature, and you can transform your appearance and your life. Having healthy, glowing skin on the outside goes hand in hand with taking care of your belly. Having the body you want means changing the way you eat and move, and staying on the right track so that you can look as young and feel as radiant as a dancer. You don't have to know how to dance—just feel that passion!

To shine with true beauty, you must first know the real, inner you—and then express it. *The Way of the Belly* is a total mind-body-spirit approach to living the good life, with a twist . . . and a shimmy, a hip circle, and a great big smile!

Make Yourself Over—the Belly Way

The Way of the Belly can suit your own particular needs. If you're unsure of where you should start, note that each chapter explores a different aspect of our approach to life, so feel free to begin wherever you want. Here's what each chapter covers:

- In Chapter 1, we show you how to get to know yourself the ancient way, using astrology, Ayurveda, and your chakras—and the not so ancient way, a video camera. These are a great foundation for taking note of changes you want to make or adding to what you already like, whether it's physical, spiritual, or emotional guidance.

- Do you want to slim down, gain more belly energy, and have the joyful, sensual passion of a dancer? If so, lighten up with our 30-day eating plan while tickling your taste buds with the exotic fare of the Middle East and India in Chapter 2. This section puts the "ooooo" in food and helps you make the best choices for your weight, health, and lifestyle.

- Listening to our inner sounds empowers us to make the right decisions in life. Chapter 3 will help you tune in to your sixth sense—that is, listen with your belly. At the same time, listening also means understanding music and rhythms. This chapter will open your world to inspirational Arabic music, rhythms, and sounds from belly-dance countries.

⁜   If you want to tighten and tone your body, look and feel sexier, free up those hips, loosen your inhibitions, and become a better, more creative lover . . . no problem! We'll help you keep the fun in fitness by offering a new exercise option that's more like playing than working out. Learn how to shake and shimmy your body, seduce with a veil, boost your confidence, and shape your midsection with the sensual moves of belly dance in Chapter 4.

⁜   Are you feeling tired and tense? Need to relax after your dance workout? Chapter 5 shows you how to pamper yourself with luxurious massage and fragrant lotions and oils. You'll discover the joys of attending a luxurious spa when you need it, as well as how to treat yourself in the comfort and affordability of your own home.

⁜   If your clothing isn't exactly making the most of what you've got, delight in the look and feel of dressing up as you've never done before with all of the ideas in Chapter 6. You'll see how easy it is to spice up your wardrobe and how much fun it is to give your closet a makeover.

⁜   Chapter 7 outlines the ways to bring out your best facial features or just have more fun with your new exotic look. You'll discover the joy and playfulness of our bold and beautifying belly-dance-inspired hair and makeup tips and tricks.

⁜   For your grand finale in Chapter 8, we'll help you learn to love your new and improved self, other people, and all that life has to offer . . . and get the love that you deserve in return.

Maybe you want to do *all* of these things! Every page of *The Way of the Belly* will help you decide what changes you want to make and then help you achieve them.

Expect Uniqueness

One of the major themes in this book is uniqueness, in you and in us. As belly dancers and identical twins, we're not your typical authors—and this is not your typical makeover book. First, you'll notice that we alternate our voices from chapter to chapter. When we first began this project, we tried to write it from a single point of view, as if we were a single person: Neena&Veena. We soon realized that didn't work for us, since sometimes we had individual experiences or different ways of looking at something. So, instead of saying "we" all the time and mashing everything together, we decided to have one of us be the main voice of each chapter and tell the story from that person's perspective—and maintain our individuality.

You'll also notice that we often use dance terminology to get our point across. That's because we're dancers through and through, and we see all of life as a dance . . . the steps and turns and movements in our work are metaphors for the steps and turns and movements in life. Just as a choreographer designs a routine, you can create and dance your own life.

This way of life will revolve around your belly, leaving you feeling sensual, beautiful, fit, womanly, and happy. When we say "belly," we often mean your actual anatomy—the muscles and physical form that you see and feel on the outside. But sometimes when we say "belly," we mean your metaphorical center—your innermost self, the core or essence of you. While most women would like to have a nice "outer belly," the belly-dance life has taught us that the "inner belly" is just as important—and that the state of one is usually a reflection of the other.

In the following chapters, we'll show you how to take years off your face and body, make the most of what you've got, flaunt it belly-dance style, and have a great time while you're doing it. You're about to begin a self-improvement plan so enjoyable that you can actually stay on it for the rest of your life! That's because you'll be playing with all five of your senses, as well as that often-ignored sixth sense: your gut or "belly" feelings. This, too, is unique.

Following *The Way of the Belly* will give your life more flash and vitality; and transform the way you look, feel, and present yourself. The great thing is that you'll see immediate changes on the outside. But as time goes by, you'll also notice deeper shifts on the inside—more confidence, joy, healthy energy, and focus—and that will make you look and feel even *more* beautiful and alluring. Be all that you have imagined you could be . . . and maybe even more. Every woman already has a belly dancer inside, so let her out! Let us inspire you and show you how.

How to Use the DVD

Belly dance is what you see, and belly-dance music is something you hear. That's why we felt that this book wouldn't be complete without a DVD. In the DVD that accompanies this book, we'll teach you the fundamental movements of belly dance as well as a routine. We'll first break down each upper-body, lower-body, and traveling steps technique separately; then, we'll show you how to put them all together into fluid, sexy choreography.

The DVD complements the belly-dance workout we'll teach you in Chapter 4, and using it will help you get a feel for doing the movements to music. But you don't need to wait until you get to that chapter to start learning the steps. You can set the book aside for a while and dive right in!

Now that you know the first and most important lesson—that you're in control, no matter what—let's get started on *The Way of the Belly*.

❋❋❋ ❋❋❋

Know Your Belly . . .
Enhance the Feminine Uniqueness in You
by Neena

Sensuality is a very good thing. Veena and I believe that *all* women are sensual, regardless of their color, size, height, or weight. This is more than what you see on a billboard or the cover of a fashion magazine, and beyond the walk of a runway model. It's attitude—your walk, your smile, how you feel about yourself and life—and the uniqueness in all of us. This ultimate feminine quality transcends all boundaries, but it can be hidden by the everyday stresses of family, home, and work. Most women end up forgetting it was ever there . . . or at best they wonder if it will ever come back!

Ladies, I'm here to tell you that your sensuality never left! It's still within you; you just have to ignite that fire inside and bring it out so that *you* can feel it and other people can *see* it.

Let's talk about how to achieve this.

My mom had a friend who, when she and her husband first got married, always wore cute clothes and makeup and styled her hair. After her second child, she gained weight and didn't bother going to the gym anymore. She said that she didn't have time because of motherhood. Soon after, I'd always see her wearing sweats and a T-shirt with her hair pulled back. Forget about makeup and jewelry. I didn't need to ask how her husband felt about her appearance, because he'd already complained about it. She automatically and defensively said, as many Indian mothers typically say, "When you're married and have kids, things change, including your body. You don't have time for yourself."

First of all, you have to be open and want to change. There's always room for improvement, no matter how much or how little. Veena and I don't want you to change or lose your sensual essence, your "inner belly" of who you are. That's the beautiful you, and you want it to be appreciated—like a work of art. All I'm saying is that we're just encouraging you to pay attention to yourself—which means attending to your hair, skin, clothes, makeup—and the way you move. All of this will heighten your awareness of who you really are and bring out the very best in you—making you more feminine and sensual the belly way. Think of this whole process as if you're dancing onstage with all eyes upon you. These are rehearsals, and we're your private coaches, directors, and choreographers.

Let's begin by setting the stage for your new life. First, begin by loving your belly. By this I mean that you need to really appreciate everything about yourself and get to know yourself the belly way. You might be thinking, *What is this Neena person talking about? I already know myself—I've been living with me all my life! I just want to . . .* [fill in the blank]. Maybe you want to be thinner, sexier, or more hip; look younger; get the right man; tone up; or feel more feminine or more beautiful. Trust me, loving your belly is an important first step.

We've transformed our own lives and have helped many others do the same—and now we hope to help you, whatever your goal is. There's always more to learn about yourself, and I hope that our suggestions will surprise and delight you. Then it will be easier for you to decide what changes you want to make, since what's good for one person isn't right for another. You need to know what it is that *you* want.

Let me reiterate that Veena and I aren't trying to make you into someone you're not. This is just our way of allowing your gifts to shine and glitter for the world to see, and this chapter is all about setting the stage for that transformation. We want to start you off on the path to your own unique destiny by first helping you discover *your* personality, strengths, desires, and preferences. This is the first step in freeing yourself to enhance your unique qualities and live the inspired, bold, sensual belly way.

Dancing Your Own Dance

People often send Veena and me e-mails saying that they want to be just like us, or even look just like us. I'm always incredibly flattered when I hear that—but our mother says that two of us is enough! And even though we're very close, we still know the value of individuality.

When Veena and I were kids, we were inseparable and each other's best friend. Our mom used to always dress us alike, so even if only one of us got our clothes dirty, she'd change both of us so that we'd always look the same. And even today, we look and act alike, and our behaviors are very similar. Yet, as is the case with most identical twins, Veena and I know that there are subtle differences between the two of us. We may share 100 percent of our genes, but we're not 100 percent the same, because we're two people who have lived somewhat different lives. We rarely had boyfriends at the same time, and even our periods aren't in sync. She's got a degree in the performing arts, and I've got a business/journalism degree. And if you look carefully, you can even notice slight differences in the shapes of our faces and our facial features.

If identical twins can be such unique individuals, then imagine how *you* stand out from the entire population! No one on earth is exactly like you. Your DNA is yours alone, along with your horoscope and your thumbprint. Your body shape, level of energy, favorite color, food preferences and requirements, posture, movement, attitude, and talents . . . all of these belong to you. *Dare* to be unique!

Our experience as professional belly dancers has taught us so much about being individuals and how to put our very best foot forward both onstage and in life. We hope to inspire you to enhance your uniqueness so that you can be your best self and express yourself individually and creatively—in everything you do. The world's a stage, and everyone is a performer. There's no right or wrong, just your interpretation of your performance. That's what belly dance, and this book, are all about: the way of *your* belly.

Transforming Your Inner and Outer Belly

My very first job was babysitting for two children both under the age of six. It was pretty fun watching them play—creatively expressing their individual selves with dance-like movements and goofy sounds. No inhibitions, no "baggage," which we as adults accumulate more and more of as we get older. Their love for life and for the world was so pure and innocent as they laughed and played. I remember when Neena and I were like that ourselves: When we were three years old, we'd play on this old swing set for what seemed to be hours almost every day. It was so much fun that the memory still makes me smile.

What Is Belly Dance?

Americans got their first taste of belly dance when the famous dancer Little Egypt danced at the 1893 World's Fair in Chicago. But belly dance is one of the oldest forms of movement and has been practiced for thousands of years. Exactly where it comes from is a bit of a mystery, but it probably has many roots in the various ancient cultures of India, the eastern Mediterranean, and the Middle East.

The hip movements are similar to those found in dances from Africa, Brazil, and Haiti; while the graceful arm gestures may have come from Asia, ancient Persia, or northern India. What we do know is that it has survived for thousands of years and is popular throughout the world today.

The name is a mystery, too. Some feel that the term *belly dance* is an insult, but others love it because it emphasizes the belly as the source of life and strength. The expression is thought to come from the French term for this type of activity, *danse du*

3

verte, which means "dance of the stomach." Another possibility is that it originated from the Middle Eastern word *beledi*, which means "my country." In academic circles and in non-English-speaking countries, it's known as Oriental Dance or *Raks Sharki*.

Regardless of its origin, some experts believe that this tradition emerged out of rituals linked to womanhood, sensuality, and fertility—which certainly seems reason-able when you look at the sensual move-ments. Maybe the women danced for each other as part of a ceremonial fertility rite, or perhaps women wise in the ways of the world taught young girls the dance as a way to prepare their bodies and minds for marriage and childbirth. To this day, the movements are often done the traditional way: barefoot, which emphasizes the intimate physical connection between the dancer and Mother Earth.

Belly dance was once performed as entertainment for royalty and common people alike. But when patriarchal religions took hold, this tradition

But as children grow older, they try to "fit in" by copying others; as adults, women often continue to surrender to the pressure to look or be like someone else. When my sister and I were in school, we wanted to belong and be like all the other kids, too. We hated being different from everyone—olive-skinned, listening to different music, and wearing secondhand clothes—that was soooo uncool.

As we grew older, however, we not only learned to accept our cultural heritage and our tough-times roots, we actually accentuated those experiences in ways that made us different from everyone else. Through belly dance, we've learned to let go of our negative interpretation of our past, and have turned it into something that made us who we are today: unique and sensual beings. This feminine dance that allows you to let yourself go and be in touch with your freedom, just as we were in childhood. As I'm dancing, I imagine the enjoyment and freedom that Veena and I had playing on that old swing set. This kind of feeling can be experienced by women of all cultural backgrounds.

Our family roots are mostly from India and Pakistan, although Veena and I were born in California. Some branches of our family came from various areas of the Middle East (mostly the Gulf region), and they still reside there. So we'll be giving you information and advice from our own cultural point of view in this book.

Although belly dance is primarily from Egypt, it's enjoyed by millions of Arabic and non-Arabic speaking people all over the world. Who would have known that this tradition enjoyed by so many would be what brought Veena and me closer to not only our own culture but also to each other? That's exactly what happened: We started becoming comfortable with how we looked, who we were, and our cultural background. And it was because of everything that this dance is about: femininity, empowerment, grace, and sensuality, which just about every woman can relate to.

Today, my sister and I embrace everything that we grew up with— even the rough times—and being confident with ourselves means that we believe in who we are inside. We've come to think of these inner selves as our "inner bellies," because the belly is not only the center of our physical bodies, but also our emotional and spiritual core.

Your inner belly is the center of the unique person that is you—who you are now and the identity that you can create. Being confident with and proud of this part of yourself helps you exude sensuality. Just as the physical belly comes in all shapes and sizes, each with its own type of beauty, so do inner bellies. You can see this in different personality traits, talents, and histories. Your inner belly is unique and beautiful . . . it's *you*.

When you really can know, appreciate, and love your "belly-self," you're building a strong foundation for deciding what changes you want to make—for yourself, not for anyone else. Knowing your belly-self is the first step toward choreographing your own life and transforming your belly, your body, and yourself; and in bringing out the more sensual, sexy you. Whether that means making it more beautiful, fit, healthy, decorated, or pampered—or all of these things—is totally up to you.

So, who are you? Let's find out.

Ways of Knowing

I learn who I am on the outside because I have a twin—even though we have subtle differences, Veena and I are identical enough to be a "reflection" of each other. I've observed her behavior, how she interacts with other people, the way she talks, the best clothes and makeup for her, and her movements—the way she gestures, walks, and yes, of course, dances. Veena is a mirror for me, in both my looks and the way I move. Without even realizing it, over the years we've become each other's teacher and student.

If you don't have a twin to clearly (or inadvertently) tell you about yourself, perhaps your sister, mother, or female best friend can help you

became evil and forbidden, no longer sacred, spiritual, healthy, or acceptable. The practice went underground, and women dancers were hired for those in the harems, minus the ritualistic or religious aspects.

Today, belly dance plays many roles in its native countries and in the nations where it has spread. Per-formers cele-brate special family and social occasions such as births, weddings, harvests, and religious holidays. It can be pure entertainment, an expressive art form, and a great way to get and stay fit.

Like life itself, belly dance is both a mystery and a delight, and it can be whatever you make of it—if you stay true to your unique self.

understand some aspects of who you really are, inside or out. It's hard to "see" yourself without some kind of mirror.

There are a lot of "mirrors" out there—tests, theories, methods, and professionals to measure and analyze personalities, preferences, strengths, weaknesses, and so on. What we've provided for you in this chapter are some simple, easy approaches that you can do yourself (or with a little help from your friends).

AYURVEDIC DOSHA:
THE INDIAN WAY OF KNOWING YOUR BELLY

In India, there's an ancient mind-body-spirit health system called *Ayurveda* (eye-your-vay-duh) which recognizes that there are three different body types called *doshas*. Everyone is made up of all three in different amounts, but usually, one type predominates.

I like this perspective because it's a great way to get to know and accept your belly and body, and to realize that each type is beautiful. Every belly has its own appeal, and each dosha type dances through life in her own style. For example, a *pitta* type might want to show off her muscular belly with clothes that bare the midriff, while *kapha* types might favor plunging necklines to make the most of their cleavage. But I'm getting ahead of myself. What follows are short summaries of the doshas:

- **Vata types** are governed by sound and touch. They're naturally slim and not muscular, with slender hips and narrow, downward-sloping shoulders. They may be either taller or shorter than average and live a rather active life. So, if you're made up mostly of vata, you'll be naturally thin and probably have a flat or even concave belly—think fashion model. But watch out! When vata types gain weight, most of it hangs out around their waists, and they can easily grow a little pooch, even when the rest of them looks thin. Vatas also tend to get bloated, which makes their bellies puff out, but it's usually due to digestive problems, not fat. Middle-eastern music fascinates vatas because of the intricate rhythms and instruments. Their physical movements can be fast, intense, and very exciting!

- **Pitta types** are visually oriented and have a medium frame along with moderately developed muscles, including their belly muscles. Physically, their movements have strength and endurance, and they move with determination—think tennis champion. So if you're mostly pitta, and you eat too much and aren't physically active, your belly will grow along with the rest of you, but it will probably be in proportion. Pittas also enjoy belly dance because of the beautiful, glitzy costumes.

❈ **Kapha types** respond to taste and smell. They're the voluptuous ones: well developed, with heavy bones, broad shoulders, and wide hips. They can be quite tall and tend to be born to lounge. If you're mostly kapha, most of your fat will be located around your hips and thighs—think earth goddess. You can have a perfectly flat belly or a nice round one, but this is more than balanced by your bottom! Kaphas gain weight most easily and may find it difficult to lose. Physically, their movements may be slow, steady, methodical, and quite graceful. They especially love belly dance because the feminine movements emphasize their curves.

YOUR ASTROLOGICAL SIGNS: THE COSMIC WAY OF KNOWING HOW TO MOVE

Do you read your daily horoscope? This is the zodiac sign that the sun was in at the time of your birth; it represents your direction and focus in life. Sun-sign profiles are just a general picture, and in our monthly e-newsletter, we always provide a short description of the sun sign for that month, with an emphasis on how its characteristics apply to eating and physical activity. In both India and the Middle East, astrology is an important part of daily living, and it's been an incredible guide in our lives as well. There are so many more details that can be understood in your own astrological profile that goes beyond just your sun sign. If you'd like an individualized picture, consider having your chart done by a knowledgeable astrologer.

Listed below are your signs and a very general description of each one's approach to belly dance, as well as other dance styles:

❈ **Capricorn** (December 22–January 19): Natural choreographer; very visual; masters new dance styles, and seeks out and creates new ones; attracted to music and rhythm.

❈ **Aquarius** (January 20–February 18): Appreciates music and dance; a great leader in group classes.

❈ **Pisces** (February 19–March 20): Creative performer; prefers dance to traditional cardio classes, and loves veils.

❈ **Aries** (March 21–April 19): Imaginative; energetic; a natural fitness buff; artistic, innovative, and creative in dance.

- **Taurus** (April 20–May 20): Prefers the structure of classical dance, such as ballet, but can be loyal followers of belly dance upon venturing out.

- **Gemini** (May 21–June 21): Needs variety in dance to keep from getting bored; fascinated by belly dance because of the variety in movement, music, and history

- **Cancer** (June 22–July 22): Creative; likes to perform in dance troupes because the other members provide motivation; a great, nurturing dance teacher.

- **Leo** (July 23–August 22): A natural and creative performer; attracted to belly dance because of the intense sensual energy.

- **Virgo** (August 23–September 22): A perfectionist with dance movements; a great dance and music instructor due to the thorough approach to technique and rhythm.

- **Libra** (September 23–October 23): Naturally artistic; a good dancer and choreographer with beautifully balanced and harmonious—yet edgy—work.

- **Scorpio** (October 24–November 21): Enjoys the passionate, sensual, and feminine aspect of belly dance, especially with the mysterious dance of the veils.

- **Sagittarius** (November 22–December 21): Naturally drawn to dance, with a strong will to master style; loves to express creativity in belly dance as a solo or group artist.

YOUR CHAKRAS:
THE ENERGETIC WAY OF KNOWING

Both Eastern and Western cultures have recognized the importance of energy for centuries, and Veena and I are all about energy—without it, we couldn't dance or do anything else that we enjoy. Whether you call it *chi*, *prana*, the life force, or whatever, it's what gives you the spark of life. It flows all through the energy centers in your body, which in Indian teachings are called *chakras*.

Everyone has the same seven chakras, but how they work together and express your unique genetic heritage is totally yours. They're the links between your physical and emotional energetic selves, and they have a powerful influence on your nerves and the hormones that affect your feelings and actions.

Chakra means "wheel" or "disk"; in Indian dance, *chakar* means "spins" or "turns." The image of the power or energy is that of a coiled snake at the base of your spine. Chakra energy spins and spirals around, creating youth and vitality, like the whirling dervish dancers from the Middle East. Chakras are both programs and memories—think of them as files that store information about your life.

The three lowest ones—those located around the belly area—are those most intensely related to your feminine physical self, so they're the ones we'll be concentrating on in this book. These centers govern deep, fundamental issues. Here's a breakdown of each one:

- **The root or first chakra** is located at the base of your spine and hips. It's affected by how safe, secure, and content you feel in the world and is associated with passion, love, sexuality, creativity, appetite, and inspiration. The body parts and systems that are associated with this chakra are your adrenal glands, lymph system, and elimination. Its element is *earth*.

- **The sacral or second chakra** is located in the belly, sexual organs, and lower back and represents emotions and memories with respect to how you relate to other people, as well as your relationship to food and sex. It governs your will, concentration, self-responsibility, and level of self-control. Its element is *water*.

- **The solar plexus or third chakra** is located just above the navel and has to do with your self-esteem, self-confidence, and self-respect. It's related to your sense of freedom and power and being comfortable with who you are. Its element is *fire*.

- **The fourth, fifth, sixth, and seventh chakras** relate to your other systems (such as your heart and circulation and your immune system) and correspond to other emotions, senses, and areas of consciousness (such as perceptions of love; and receiving acceptance, direction, and intuition).

Thinking about the chakras helps you get to know the relationship between your body, emotions, and consciousness. The centers and your physical being become a kind of map of your emotional self, giving you clues as to what's right for you. Your personality traits and even a weight problem could be related to your chakras. For example, when your first chakra isn't balanced, you may feel restless and irritable; and when your second chakra is unbalanced, you may feel burned-out, dominating, and have poor digestion.

With its undulations, hip drops, and hip shimmies (which we'll teach you in Chapter 4), belly dance strongly stimulates and balances these grounded chakras; belly breathing (also discussed in Chapter 4) tends to influence the upper chakras.

Your Color Preferences: The Colorful Way of Knowing

Asking "What's your favorite color?" is an old party game, but color psychology is a real science. Your preferences can reveal personality traits, emotional issues, and mood; they can communicate unspoken messages. Color plays a huge role in the choices you make in your clothing, makeup, and surroundings; and later in this book, we'll talk about what looks good on you. For now, let's examine what color *reveals* about you. When people look at your outward appearance, are you sending the message you want?

- **Red** means sexual pleasure, anger, risk-taking, purpose in life, and passion.
- **Red-orange** means freedom, playfulness, creativity, and spontaneity.
- **Orange** means self-esteem, assertiveness, self-love, and confidence.
- **Yellow** means hopeful, flexible, in control, empowered, optimistic, and able to let go.
- **Yellow-green** means peaceful, accepting, and unity with others.
- **Green** means love, fulfilled affection, and inspired.
- **Blue-green** means wholeness, harmony, and self-awareness.
- **Blue** means joy, expressiveness, independence, and communication.
- **Blue-violet** means understanding, clarity, insight, inner peace, and orderly thinking.
- **Violet** means trustful, visionary, spiritual, or religious.

Close Encounters

And now we come to the next step. . . . Ask your friends, relatives, and/or co-workers to describe your physical self and your personality—your inner and outer belly. Encourage honesty, because it's fascinating to hear what others notice. Sometimes people pick up on things that you don't see yourself, both "good" and "bad." For example, they may point out that you wear a heavy perfume versus a light fragrance, if you have fresh breath, if your hands are soft when you shake their hand, if your clothes are neat and clean, and so forth.

Try asking that same question of your spouse or lover. What matters to you may not register at all on their radar—and vice versa. Sometimes you might be projecting an image of who you want to be, and it helps to know what's really being put out there and how that compares with who you think you are.

Now take a look at all of these impressions of your inner and outer self. It's amazing how much of what's in you bubbles up to the surface as an outward expression of what's going on inside. Do others perceive you differently than you see yourself—or in some way other than how you *want* to be seen?

Bellies, Truth, and Videotape

Up till now we've given you several ways of knowing yourself, each with its own perspective and way of blending the characteristics of the inner and outer you. Maybe you prefer one approach over another, but they all give you some ideas about how much variety there is in people. The next step is to take yet another look at yourself as you prepare for your big performance—it's like the first day of rehearsal.

Let's start by standing in front of a full-length mirror, and looking at yourself from head to toe. How would you generally describe yourself?

Let's take it a step further. Get your video camera (or borrow one) and set it up on a tripod, or ask a friend to be your camera person. Go to your closet and get three of your favorite outfits, and one at a time model each of them for the camera, full makeup and all. As you wear them, try to capture a full-body shot of yourself as you walk toward the camera. Stop about five feet from it, do a 180-degree turn, and then walk away, showing your backside; turn and face the lens again.

After the third outfit, stand in front of the camera and just talk. Say anything you wish—what you had for dinner last night, where you plan to go on your next vacation, talk about your kids or friends . . . anything.

Videotape yourself again—but this time strip down to your underwear or a bathing suit. Take that walk again. Stop, turn, and talk, either standing or sitting in front of the camera.

Now play back the tape and watch. If you've never seen yourself on video, you may be a little surprised by how you appear. I remember the first time that Veena and I saw ourselves on television, I said, "That doesn't look like me! I look different when I see myself in the mirror." That's when I realized that we may not be objective about ourselves.

As you watch yourself in each of your outfits, notice the fit. Do they flatter and enhance your best features? What about the colors? Do they make you look and feel confident, energetic, and vibrant or dull and insecure? Does your hair frame or hide your face? What does the makeup say about you?

Now watch your "bare" self and describe your movements. Is your walk confident or tense? Take a look at your feet: Are they turned out like a duck or pigeon-toed and turned in?

Your posture also tells people how you carry yourself: The way you sit, stand, and walk says a lot about your self-confidence, self-esteem, and energy levels. Check your shoulders—are they curved forward, or is one higher than the other? Notice whether you look straight ahead or down, and if your chin is jutting forward. Are you slumping or swaybacked? When you sit, do you collapse or fold in on yourself? The video doesn't lie! (You'll learn how to improve and enhance your posture in Chapter 4.)

Try reviewing the tape again. How would you describe your outer belly—your general shape, color, clothing, hair, and makeup? What about your inner belly—your general attitude, energy level, sincerity, and confidence? Note the changes you'd like to make.

Start Making Sense and Making Over

Okay, ladies, now that you've started to figure out who you are, it's time for a feminine makeover the belly way! If you want to . . .

※ Improve your physical appearance

※ Lose weight by burning calories, decreasing food cravings, and boosting metabolism

※ Charge up your energy levels

※ Relax and get your beauty sleep

※ Perk up and even out your mood

※ Increase your confidence and self-esteem

※ Make all of your body systems work better—including your immune, endocrine, reproductive, circulatory, and digestive systems

* Boost your brainpower and memory

* Improve your posture

* Improve your muscle tone and flexibility

* Reduce your risk of many serious diseases

* Be a better lover

* Look and feel younger

. . . then you're on the proper path to a feminine makeover, described in detail in the remaining chapters! You see, all of our senses are working 24/7, taking in information for our brains and inner bellies to process. Belly dance has a bold effect on everything we perceive, which makes the experience so powerful and enjoyable. With the bright lights, colorful costumes, eye-catching makeup, mesmerizing movements, exotic music, and flirtatious finger cymbals, belly dance is a sensory extravaganza . . . that's why it's such a sensual delight.

You are a total sensory experience, too. Our program will have you paying attention to all of your senses—touch, feel, sound, sight, and smell. Enjoying your touch and being touched; discovering how you tune in to your needs and to others'; transforming yourself visually; listening to exotic music; and smelling the sweet aroma of everything, including your own unique fragrance and delicious, healthy foods, may be exactly what you need. What you're taking in, and what you're projecting out into the world, will be the new you . . . with a feminine, sensory makeover for the world to enjoy.

Maybe you're totally happy with the way you are right now—that's great, too! In the following chapters, Veena and I will show you how to make the most of what you've got, and to flaunt it belly-dance style. No matter what aspect of yourself you want to improve or just accentuate, we'll help you make those changes.

We want to bring out your own unique, beautiful, and sensual gifts. The most important thing that you can do now is *decide* to make those changes, *be ready* to make them, and *be committed* to doing what it takes to achieve your goals (and we'll make that part easy for you).

You'll use all of your senses as you create the new you—from perhaps changing your body shape by eating right and exercising (both of which can be very sensual), to maybe making better choices in colors and/or clothes (just think of the richness of hues and textures to see and feel!). With each step you take to move yourself closer to your goals, you'll gain self-respect, and people around you will notice your confidence and gravitate to you. The world will become your stage, and you'll be the star performer!

First, let's clear the decks and lighten up your eating habits so that you can perform at your very best.

*** ***

Chapter Two

LIGHTEN YOUR BELLY . . .
30 DAYS TO A DANCER'S BODY
BY VEENA

So many people ask us how we stay slim and have so much energy to dance. Well, it's really pretty simple: We get our bodies and our energy from the way we eat. Believe it or not, one of the secrets of our success is that we eat six meals a day! (Okay, so they're small ones. . . .) That's why, if you want to feel lighter and shed those extra pounds that are weighing you down, we recommend that you don't go on a traditional "diet." Instead, experience a new, lighter way of eating that will keep your belly happy, healthy, and give you enough energy to dance all day (and all night!).

Let's face it—"diets" often don't work. They can deprive you of your favorite dishes without offering a delicious, healthful substitution. You know what you *can't* have, but what *can* you eat—boring, flavorless foods eaten in an unnatural way? You often have to continually count calories and measure grams. Who has time for that? And under these regimes, food isn't enjoyable anymore, so it's no wonder that most people can't stay on them for very long. What's more, diets can actually be unhealthy and destroy your energy and metabolism. It's hard to shimmy when you're feeling weak and grouchy!

So don't worry. I'm not talking about extremes like subsisting on a diet of bean sprouts and nonfat cottage cheese, completely vegetarian, only meat, or food that tastes like watered-down cardboard. Nope, I'm talking about another kind of extreme-eating makeover: a menu that aims for freshness and is close to nature, including satisfying nuts, creamy avocados, fresh fish, baked potatoes, luscious peaches, juicy melons, colorful berries, chewy grains, crunchy salads, and even the occasional dark-chocolate or coconut treat. I'm talking about freedom from counting grams or calories—neither Neena nor I have ever tracked any of these in our lives. And you'll be happy to hear that we're going to teach you a simple way of eating that actually improves the condition of your skin and hair, increases your energy level, and elevates your mood and your health so that you can enjoy your new dancer's body even more.

Welcome to Neena & Veena's Happy-Belly Café

I don't want you to even *think* the word *diet*—just get it out of your vocabulary. (Lighten your mind before you lighten your belly!) Instead, think of our nutrition plan as eating in Neena & Veena's Happy-Belly Café. Our place serves you foods that are naturally delicious and satisfying, and dishes full of variety and spice that will rock your taste buds and please your belly. Food should be a joyful and sensual experience, caressing every part of your tongue—not a chore! In some ways, our delicious way of eating harkens back to our Indian and Middle Eastern roots, but it doesn't stop there. We'll also help you navigate your way safely through the kitchen, as well as real-world cafés and many types of ethnic restaurants. (Take a look at our menu in the Appendix.)

Read on and you'll find our one-month kickoff program to get you started, which includes a super fat-melting grapefruit one-day fast. In the second month, we'll give you some additional advice to fine-tune your new way of eating and experiencing food. Then we'll send you on your way to a lifelong program of delicious eating that will keep your weight and energy level where you want so that you're ready for anything!

With this new way of eating, you might see some changes immediately; others will take some time. When you approach food in the way that Neena and I do (even if you don't really want or need to lose weight), you'll feel lighter, sexier, and more energetic. And if you *do* want to shed some extra pounds, you'll lighten up and lose weight painlessly. When you eat nutritious food in the proper amounts, your body will naturally drop weight and eliminate flab where it's supposed to. It's okay to check your progress every now and then on your bathroom scale, but don't get obsessed with those numbers. Neena and I prefer to keep tabs on how our clothes fit and how we feel, rather than only judging our weight by the numbers.

The Bellytwins' Four-Week Lighten-Up Nutritional Program

This is a four-week program. The first day of each week, you'll be going through your refrigerator, freezer, pantry, and cupboards and throwing away foods that don't belong inside your belly because they're unhealthy. That same day, you'll be making a trip to the grocery store or farmers' market and shopping in food aisles that you might never have visited before. The rest of that week, you'll be changing one thing about the way you're eating now so that you *gradually* shift toward a lighter, healthier way of eating.

There's no need to rush and bite off more than you can chew. Take one step at a time, as if you were learning a whole new type of choreography . . . a dance of eating! Practice what you learn each week, and don't worry if you make a "mistake." Just keep going, and pat yourself on the back when you see progress.

What follows are the basics for the first four weeks. But if you're gung ho about losing extra fat, or if you want to detoxify your system so that your engine can run better—or both—we recommend that while you're making these four changes, you also do a grapefruit fast (see page 27) once a week, or at least once a month.

Okay, let's get started!

Week 1: Change Your Drinking Habits

- Throw out sodas, iced teas, fruit punches, and other beverages containing sugar and caffeine.
- Get filtered water, or buy a water filter that purifies tap water.
- Drink at least eight glasses of water a day.

This is such a simple, yet powerful, change, especially if you're watching your weight. Water not only fills you up, but it has zero calories, sugar, salt, caffeine, and alcohol—zero artificial anything. It flushes out your system, has no side effects, and it's cheap!

Neena and I drink a lot of water throughout the day, and we usually carry a water bottle around with us wherever we go. Because we're very physically active, we need to regularly replace what we've lost through sweating. Fortunately, these days, you can get pure water just about anywhere. And whether we're in a restaurant or at a gym, we sometimes spruce up an ordinary glass of water by adding a packet of Emer'gen-C to our glasses of water. It adds fizz and flavor and gives us extra vitamin C—it's an instant "sports" drink!

Many people—including a lot of our friends and family—gotta have their coffee, soda, alcohol, or afternoon chai. I know it's really hard to let go of these beverages altogether, so wean yourself slowly, or at least try to cut back. Sure, caffeine may have some benefits, such as instant energy and giving you a reason to hang out at Starbucks with your friends. But just remember, too much in your system can dehydrate your skin, decrease collagen levels, and lead to premature wrinkling. And if you're ingesting a lot of caffeine or sodas, you're probably not consuming enough water.

Also, go easy on the alcohol. Too much is a stress on the liver, and drinking really puts on the pounds. You'll be surprised by how those calories add up! A friend of ours who loved her margaritas felt that she was a little pudgy and wanted to trim down. So she cut her alcohol intake to only one to two drinks a day, and she *immediately* lost the extra weight. Now, because she takes in more water, her belly has never felt better.

WEEK 2: MAKE FRUITS AND VEGETABLES YOUR BEST FRIENDS

- Throw away cookies, candies, and pastries.
- Buy organic fruits and vegetables.
- Continue drinking plenty of water.

Aim to eat at least five fresh fruits and vegetables every day, emphasizing the veggies. This is the best thing you can do to reduce calories without counting them. These foods are high in water and fiber to fill you up; and packed with vitamins, minerals, and other nutrients to help your body burn fat, stay healthy, and dance with lots of life.

Try to get plenty of variety, and include at least one salad daily. There are hundreds of different varieties of produce out there, and more are becoming available all the time, thanks to our multicultural society.

Of course, when I recommend that you stock up on these foods, I don't mean canned peaches in syrup or deep-fried potatoes! Go for the fresh and raw stuff, and if you can, go organic. Neena and I love to buy fruits and veggies in a rainbow of colors as bright and beautiful as our costumes: green, red, orange, yellow, blue, purple, and white. And the more colorful something is, then the more beautiful it appears on your plate, and the more nutritious it is.

Eat veggies raw, or cook them lightly with little or no fat: steamed, baked, stir-fried, boiled in a little water or broth, in soups, or in stews. It's really easy to add these choices to your day: Just keep the fruits and vegetables on hand for snacking. Instead of reaching for a Gummi Bear or a bag of corn chips, how about a juicy plum, bright red cherry tomatoes, or sweet and crunchy jicama? If it's extra zing we're after, Neena and I often squeeze a little lemon juice or sprinkle some paprika over our snacks; and I like a little cayenne pepper and sea salt on my Granny Smith apple. Try it—you might be surprised!

Week 3: Give Yourself an Oil Change

⊠ Throw away all items containing unhealthy fats and rancid or old oils.

⊠ Buy foods containing healthy fats.

⊠ Continue drinking water and eating fruits and vegetables.

"Fat?!" one of my friends exclaimed. "But I want to *lose* weight!" Believe it or not, your body actually needs fats to stay healthy and to keep your skin smooth and moist and your hair silky, shiny, and sexy. These substances are also good for your brain (specifically, intelligence and memory), and they're very satisfying. Include a little healthy fat in your meal and you won't get that empty feeling so quickly.

One time just before Neena and I were about to appear on a live television talk show with a studio audience, my belly started grumbling. It could have been an embarrassing moment, because those microphones pick up all kinds of sounds! So I grabbed a handful of raw almonds and was good to go for our appearance—and I didn't worry for a moment about nuts being high in fat or calories.

However, there are healthy and unhealthy choices for this food group. Most Americans indulge in a high-fat diet, and most of it is in a form that's not healthy. For example, Neena's housekeeper, Rosa, once asked my sister what her secret was for staying slim. Rosa explained that she had a good diet, eating only small portions of meat, a lot of beans, and a good amount of fruits and vegetables. After discovering that Rosa used lard in her beans, Neena suggested cutting that ingredient out completely. Within several weeks, she lost 15 pounds, doing nothing else different! So keep in mind that it's not just *how much* fat you're eating, it's *what kind* that's also important. To help you out, here are some guidelines:

⊠ **Healthy fats:** When we choose our fats, we emphasize those found in plant sources such as nuts, avocados, and vegetable oils (such as olive, sunflower, and canola oil). We add hemp-seed, flaxseed, or grape-seed oil to salads and cooked foods; and we cook with a small amount of extra-virgin coconut oil or *ghee* (Indian-style clarified butter). We also get some fats from fish; salmon is my favorite.

⊠ **Unhealthy fats:** Whenever possible, we avoid fats found in meat, whole-milk dairy products (such as cheese, milk, and ice cream), poultry skin, and egg yolks. Some plant foods are also high in unhealthy fats, including coconut oil that has been altered from its original form (usually found in commercial candy bars), palm oil, and palm-kernel oil. We also avoid trans fats, which are found in commercially prepared baked goods, margarines, snack foods, and processed foods. Commercially prepared fried dishes (such as French fries and onion rings) also contain a good deal of trans fats. These substances are extremely bad for our nervous systems, blood vessels, and bellies!

WEEK 4: SWITCH TO HEALTHY GRAINS

⬚ Throw away everything that contains white (or refined) anything, such as white flour, white rice, and artificial ingredients.

⬚ Buy whole and sprouted grains, such as brown rice, steel-cut oatmeal, and quinoa.

⬚ Continue drinking water and eating fruits, vegetables, and healthy fats.

By *refined,* I mean most breads, crackers, cakes, cookies, and cold cereals. Don't be fooled by labels that say "wheat" bread but contain mostly white flour and food coloring; read them carefully, like a detective. From the age of five, I've always found labels to be fascinating, like a small recipe on each can or jar. That's a habit I picked up from my mom, who used to always compare the ingredients of name brands to cheaper ones.

Like your new best friends, your fruits, vegetables, and whole grains contain lots of fiber to fill you up and keep you regular, along with ample metabolism-friendly nutrients. They're also a great source of carbohydrates, which are the most efficient, cleanest-burning source of energy for all the cells of your body (important for dancers), including those in your brain.

Neena and I have whole, unprocessed grains a couple of times a day. One of my regular favorites is sprouted wheat or multiseed bread—it's delicious, naturally sweet, very satisfying, and allergen-free. I also often enjoy cooked cereals (such as quinoa flakes, oatmeal, and grits) jazzed up with pine nuts, almonds, or walnuts. One of my favorite cooked grains is amaranth, because it tastes like the religious food offering, or *prasad,* at the Indian Sikh temple. Other favorites include brown rice (brown-rice crackers are Neena's favorite!), polenta, spelt, barley, buckwheat, amaranth, and Kamut wheat—I love all their the nutty flavors and chewy textures. Most important, they give me sustained energy, not a sugar rush followed by a crash.

Eating from the Neena & Veena Menu

Some of our fellow dancers wonder why Neena and I still continue to eat the way we do. They ask, "You don't need to lose any weight, so why be on a diet?"

We're not dieting; we're nourishing our bellies so that we can dance and perform at the optimal level. Because when we perform well, we feel good; and when we feel good, we look good. That's sensual, just like belly dance. We want you to feel the same so that you can perform at your very best, whatever it is, whether it's being the CEO of a company or a stay-at-home mom.

Neena and I have been eating this way for so long that it's practically second nature to us. But we understand that you might need a little help at first. So in addition to all of the tips in this chapter, we're giving you a sample menu (see the Appendix) to give you an idea of how we eat and to get you started. Whether you're putting your meals together at home or dining out, why not eat from our selection for one week and see how you feel? You won't be bored or hungry, and you'll feel great!

If you follow our pattern of eating five or six times a day, remember to keep those portions relatively small. Eating frequent "mini-meals" is really the key to losing weight, and you won't feel hungry. Neena and I have seen firsthand how starvation doesn't work: A dancer friend of ours would gulp a big cup of coffee for breakfast, and have just a tiny bite of food now and then for the rest of the day. She couldn't understand why she felt so tired and wasn't losing weight. It was clear to me that because she was eating so little, her body had switched gears and gone into "starvation mode." Her metabolism had slowed way down, and her cells held on to every calorie she consumed. To burn fat, you need to "stoke the fire" and nourish yourself to reassure your body that you're not starving. Your body needs food to perform!

FIND YOUR OWN PACE

It's hard for many people to completely cut out certain foods or beverages, so they find themselves reverting to old habits. If this is true for you, break each of the four weeks' tasks that we just discussed into smaller baby steps so that you're more gradually working your way toward change. We understand that it's hard to break habits you've had all your life.

Some years ago, Neena decided to stop having soda and to start drinking more water. Even though she wasn't downing that many soft drinks by any standard, she realized that she had a problem with sugar and wanted to eliminate this particular source of it from her life. So she started by switching to a naturally sweetened version as her first change. Then, after about one month, she took the next step: She switched to mineral water mixed with orange juice. The following month, she replaced the juice with a twist of lemon; and finally, she walked away from carbonation and started drinking plain water with a little lemon in it.

In this way, she painlessly weaned herself away from something that she knew wasn't doing her any good. I recommend that you follow her example: Take small steps and look for attractive replacements. For example, instead of extra-rich double-chocolate-nut-brownie ice cream, switch to the low-fat variety, then low-fat yogurt, and maybe even nondairy versions eventually . . . and so on. If you're a coffee drinker, try moving to organic, then water-processed decaf or black tea, ending up with green or herbal tea.

Know your body and how far you can go, but do keep pushing yourself. You might surpass your perceived limits—and you may be pleasantly surprised by how tasty the healthy alternatives are.

TIPS FOR FINE-TUNING YOUR EATING HABITS

After a month of eating our way, you'll notice immediate changes in yourself: You'll be lighter, more energetic, feel more like a dancer; and you'll probably drop a few pounds or inches, too. You'll be ready to perform and be lighter on your feet—and off of them (wink, wink). You'll *want* to continue your healthy habits, so once you know the basics of the belly way to eat and have had the chance to incorporate them into your life for a month, it's time to take it a little further and fine-tune things a bit.

The following tips may not all be directly related to immediate weight loss, but they'll eventually help you lose unwanted fat in a healthy way. Keep up the good work of the first four weeks, and when the end of the first month rolls around, think about these things as well:

Always be ready to dance. Keep your portions small enough that you wouldn't feel uncomfortable if you were to get up and start to shimmy and twirl. Eat enough to nourish yourself, but not so much that you can't do hip circles.

Timing is everything. Basically, this means that you should eat when you're hungry. Neena and I have small meals or snacks about every two to three hours, for a total of about five or six meals a day (but who's counting?!). If we're not hungry after three hours, we know that we probably ate too much at our last meal. So eat just until you're satisfied and your belly feels good, but not overly full.

There's no need to rush. Eat slowly and chew your food well. Did you know that it takes your brain 20 minutes to realize you're satisfied? Therefore, if you gulp meals in 10 minutes, you're bound to overeat, so slow down. That way, your taste buds will really enjoy every morsel.

Give your metabolism an extra edge. Eating late, just before lights out, is bad for your digestion and clogs up your system. So basically, we want you to avoid eating at midnight. Yeah, we know, having those chic late-night dinners is cool. It's soooo New York, Rome, and Tokyo—and very Cairo, too! But this little habit is also fattening and unhealthy. If you're ravenous at night after you've already had dinner, try a belly-healthy snack from our menu (see page 149) a couple of hours before going to bed. But no seven-course meals!

Eat it raw. Neena and I include plenty of raw foods in our diet: salads, vegetables, fruits, coconut, nuts, seeds, and sprouted grains. Raw ingredients are generally easier to digest than cooked food, and they give your energy levels a boost since the nutrients and enzymes haven't been altered by heat. Raw-food restaurants have become hip and offer everything from fresh fruit and vegetable juices and smoothies to elegant multicourse meals. In fact, some of our favorite dishes are "uncooked." You can also find raw food "cookbooks" with versions of your favorite dishes, from soups to desserts.

　　If you just can't manage to eat your vegetables on their own more than every once in a while, go ahead and stop at a juice bar for a quick and easy raw-vegetable-juice "meal." Sometimes I even have one for breakfast!

Avoid artificial sweeteners. Even though too much sugar is a no-no, we don't recommend artificial sweeteners as alternatives because they're just that: artificial. They have little taste and no nutritional value. Instead, allow your taste buds to indulge in natural substitutes such as raw honey, maple syrup, maple crystals, molasses, bee pollen, stevia, and agave . . . the list goes on and on. These actually contain nutrients and have a rich flavor that goes beyond just sweet. For those who still want the taste of white sugar, I recommend organic cane juice or turbinado sugar.

AFTER-DINNER INDULGENCES

Nature has given us plenty of sweet fruits, grains, and even vegetables (such as carrots, sweet potatoes, and beets) to satisfy a sweet tooth. Sure, a rich mocha cheesecake or a piece of baklava still looks good to me sometimes, but now that Neena and I are used to not having much sugar, I just take one or two bites and my cravings are completely satisfied—and I don't feel guilty. But if I want to indulge a little more in those "forbidden" desserts, pure dark chocolate is my passion. It's rich, smooth, and soooo sensual that even a small amount is "mmmm" satisfying.

Neena and I discovered pure chocolate when we were in Europe. An older woman from Switzerland was selling her homemade goodies made of untainted, natural ingredients with no filler. She said that this was the chocolate God intended for all lovers to have, and to that we say, "Amen!"

Believe it or not, chocolate contains flavonoids, which are strong antioxidants also found in berries, red wine, and green tea. I discovered that many of our favorite health-food stores sell chocolate similar to what my sister and I had in Europe, so it's easy to pick up a good-for-you treat.

If you're not a chocolate person, there are other great alternatives to those heavy pies and pastries. Instead of desserts with lots of fat, cream, white sugar, or artificial sweeteners, how about tofu- or rice-based vanilla ice cream? You could also try lemon pudding naturally sweetened with maple crystals; moist, wheat-free carrot cake; or chewy oatmeal cookies.

Of course, not all indulgences are in the dessert category. On those special occasions when I drink, red wine is one of my favorites. While I'm a merlot person, Neena is a little more of a cabernet girl. One glass is the perfect accompaniment to your meal while dining with that special man in your life, since every sip is like a sensual kiss from nature, and makes your taste buds dance. Neena and I both prefer our wine to be organic and sulfite-free. These types have all the benefits without the extra preservatives or sugar, and it feels good in my belly.

If alcohol isn't an option for you, it doesn't mean that you have to stay away from clubs or parties. While everyone else is ordering a glass of sugar-and-alcohol calories, just flash a sexy smile and request some hip, designer water in a wine glass with a squeeze of lemon, or a sparkling water mixed with a little fruit juice, as Neena and I usually do. Sometimes, I order just fruit juice and dress it up with a little salt around the rim of the glass, with a twist of citrus. It just looks like a "night-out-on-the-town" drink, and lets me dance all night if I want to, without the after morning hang-over.

One-Day Grapefruit Fast

What—just eat grapefruit? That's right: Have only grapefruit for one day, as many as you want (plus pure water). That's it! This simple step will knock off some weight and leave you lighter and more energized immediately. We've eaten as many as eight grapefruits in one day. If we're on the road, we can just take them with us.

I enjoy all grapefruit, but Neena and I both love the ruby-red variety best—it's so naturally sweet and flavorful. If we're at home and not rushing, we'll section the fruit and eat it with a spoon, savoring every morsel. If we're on the go, we'll just take our supply along with us and peel them like oranges.

Fresh, ripe grapefruits are awesome and taste great just the way they are: naked. So eat them plain, with no sugar sprinkled on top (although I do like to throw on a dash of sea salt sometimes). And it's better not to juice them; the pulp and rind have enzymes that are beneficial, and the fiber will help fill you up.

We've been doing weekly one-day grapefruit fasts for years now. Twenty-four hours is all you need for your belly to feel rejuvenated, trim, and lighter. Neena likes to fast on Sunday, while I prefer Wednesday because it falls in the middle of the week, and also because our great-grandmother used to fast on that day. *"Bood Kum Sood . . . ,"* she used to say, which means "Good things are destined to happen on Wednesdays."

Wouldn't it be great to take the whole day off and make it a spa day? Eat a grapefruit and watch the sunrise. Eat a grapefruit and go for a walk in the park or along the beach. Eat a grapefruit and get a massage, facial, manicure, or pedicure. Eat a grapefruit and watch the sunset. Eat a grapefruit and meditate and cleanse your mind.

You might want to take it easy and use the day to reflect and chill out, or you can fit in a low-key movement class if you feel like it. Go to bed early and wake up with a lighter, rested, and rejuvenated belly, body, and soul. Grapefruit fasting is easy, simple, inexpensive, and convenient—and as a bonus, you'll have a whole day with no cooking, food decisions, or dishes to wash!

People often ask us "Why grapefruit?" We tell them that it has a long history as a diet food and fat burner, and recent studies show that the benefits of eating this food aren't myths. It actually does help you lose weight. Grapefruit is not only delicious, it's soooo healthy, since it contains natural chemicals that help regulate the blood-sugar hormone, insulin. This helps your belly process food better and prevents it from being deposited as fat. What's more, it's chock-full of vitamin C, fiber, and other phytochemicals that may help prevent colds, cancer, and heart disease. In fact, grapefruit is so close to a miracle food that if you want to, it's a good idea to eat one every day, even when you're not fasting. It really will help keep those pounds from creeping up on you.

However, if you don't like grapefruit or they don't agree with you, you can substitute another fruit containing lots of fiber and water—such as oranges, apples, pineapples, papayas, or mangoes (but not bananas)—but just know that you won't get quite the same fat-burning effect.

Supplements: A Little Help from Our Friends

Believe it or not, Neena and I also take nutritional supplements, because we don't believe that we can live in this modern world and get everything that we need from food the way it's produced today. *Supplements are especially important to help you control your weight.* After all, you want your body to have all the building blocks it needs to metabolize food and burn fat.

You'll be eating foods that are rich in vitamins and minerals, but to be on the safe side, consider taking at least a basic multivitamin and mineral supplement. Every morning, we also take green powders, which contain dehydrated grass juice, chlorella, vitamins, minerals, and micronutrients—very rejuvenating and cleansing. Even the prestigious publication *The Journal of the American Medical Association* now recommends supplements. We look very closely at the labels to make sure that they don't have yeast or fillers or sugars, or things that we could be allergic to.

Note: Before adding grapefruit to your diet, check with your heath-care provider to see if you're taking any medication that might be affected. If you have diabetes, you should also check with your doctor first.

Getting Organic: In the Greenroom

When Neena and I were kids, we had a walnut tree, a cherry tree, and other fruit trees right outside our house. Often we would pick the nuts and fruits and eat them right off the tree. These foods were simple yet filling (and free!).

Today, before a performance we often find ourselves backstage in "the greenroom" (the lounging room for TV-show guests) with a spread of food containing a variety of raw fruits, vegetables, nuts, and some other stuff not on the Neena & Veena menu! Yet, the different fruits and veggies always take me back to childhood. They're such satisfying perfect foods, and one piece of fruit or a handful of nuts gives me so much energy before a performance.

These days, television producers understand that many of their guests are watching their weight and their health, so more and more fresh fruits and vegetables are appearing on the food trays. The greenroom has been greened!

Just as my sister and I used to pluck fruit from our trees, you can also harvest from your own orchard. You may not have your own farm, but no matter—seasonal foods that are grown close to home are naturally fresher (and therefore more nutritious) than those that have been stored for months or shipped for thousands of miles. So, fill your shopping basket with fresh, local, seasonal, organic foods.

We prefer to eat organic foods because of our concern about artificial fertilizers, pesticides, and other growth enhancers. Besides, organic produce is more nutritious, tastes better, and improves our energy! And because it lightens the toxic load on your digestion and metabolism, it may give your weight-loss efforts a boost. Some people consider fresh organic foods a luxury, but there are plenty of greengrocers and farmers' markets cropping up all over the cities and suburbs. Neena and I have a great time at the farmers' market—it reminds us of going to the local markets in India and the Middle East, picking the freshest local produce.

Some foods are more important to buy organic than others. Tomatoes, for example, tend to readily absorb any chemicals that have been sprayed on them. Strawberries, rice, corn, bananas, green beans, peaches, apples, and root vegetables may be particularly contaminated and thus more important to buy organic. If that just isn't going to happen for you, at least thoroughly wash and peel them (if possible) before eating.

Getting Philosophical: Eating for Your Own Belly

Neena and I consider ourselves vegans, vegetarians, and yes, meat eaters. We eat what we feel our bellies tell us to; that is, what feels right for us on that day, at that time. When you look at our menu (see page 149), you'll see that we eat a variety of foods, as long as they're prepared with a loving belly in mind.

People are often surprised to hear that we sometimes choose meat, because we were raised vegetarians for the first few years of our lives. Since our family was poor and hailed from India, a vegetarian lifestyle was not only less expensive, but a religious way of life for us. When Neena and I were kids, we got all our protein from plant foods, especially nuts and beans. But over the years, we both realized that we'd occasionally crave a little meat and fish, but not a lot of it—in fact, very little of it. But eating animal protein didn't make us feel wrong or less spiritual, because we honor and cherish all foods with a prayer before each meal. And although our bellies love and even prefer vegetables, we don't deny ourselves some animal protein when it feels right. For our particular bellies, a little salmon, lamb, or turkey is beneficial; for others, it may be chicken, beef, or other types of meat (which doesn't mean that it's okay to eat an entire cow at every meal!).

If you decide to add more of certain individual supplements, be sure that you don't get too high a dose. For information on how to design your own vitamin and mineral program, contact your physician and/or a health expert. (Also see *The Real Vitamin & Mineral Book;* and for information about herbs and other natural supplements for weight loss see *Dare to Lose*—both of which are by Dr. Shari Lieberman and Nancy Bruning, our co-author.) Keep in mind, however, that vitamins aren't a replacement for a good diet.

29

Small amounts of certain meats, poultry, and fish may be good for your belly type. Nuts, seeds, beans, and lentils, are also good for my sister and me, and these are a major source of protein for us today. Our general rule is that on days that we eat meat, our plates contain about 20 to 25 percent meat (around four ounces), and the rest is vegetables.

A large portion of meat is heavy, difficult to digest, and often rich in fat, but a small amount won't have the same negative effect. Most of us could—and should—lighten up on these foods. I'm always amazed at the portions of meat, poultry, and fish that are still being served in most restaurants, so a lot of times, Neena and I split one of these dishes two (or even three) ways, and order lots of veggie side dishes. If you're not dining with a twin, your mate, or a friend, just take the rest of your meat home in a doggie bag for another meal.

I know lots of other people who don't feel well eating a strictly vegetarian diet either, even if it's perfectly designed by a nutritionist. When they start eating meat again, their bodies become transformed and their energy begins flowing properly. So be a vegetarian if your own belly guides you to do so, not because a yogi, a friend, or an animal-rights organization tells you to. And if you've been eating vegetarian and have gained weight or lost energy, don't beat yourself up over being a carnivore. If you *are* a meat eater, try to stick with organic, vegetarian-fed, and/or free-range poultry.

Milk is one of the most common foods in the dairy world. Even though it has some advantages, Neena and I have found that our bellies don't quite agree with it for the most part. In fact, many bellies are the same way. Whole milk contains "bad fats," which affect the smoothness of our skin and leads to flabby bellies. I like this beverage, but Neena and I actually prefer almond milk over cow's milk, which we've found hard to digest for our bodies. I like the light nutty taste of this alternative, and it doesn't make my nose stuffy.

So if you feel uncomfortable after drinking milk or eating cheese or other dairy products, try switching to other types of milk, including almond, oat, soy, or rice milk, and see how you feel. Sometimes I drink a little goat's milk, which has a similar taste to cow's milk, and it's easier to digest. But if you love the standard type of dairy, try organic, raw varieties that are low- or nonfat.

Getting Real: Adapting Your Favorites

What about indulging in your favorite recipes, traveling, eating in restaurants, going to parties, and celebrating holidays? Believe me, it's quite possible to eat this new way, no matter what; you just need to be creative. You don't have to change everything at once, and you can enjoy special foods near and dear to your heart (even chocolate!) occasionally. I don't think that anything should be totally off-limits, otherwise you may find yourself not eating at all while trying to adjust to this new style of nutrition.

If you have a problem digesting, or you have an allergy to certain foods, then it's best to eliminate the item entirely, at least temporarily. But that doesn't mean you have to throw out all of your cookbooks and favorite dishes or give up your regular restaurants. You can still have your cake (made differently), and eat it, too.

COOKING MAKEOVER

When I was five years old, I loved helping my mom in the kitchen, and at the age of seven, I cooked some dishes for our family all by myself. By the time I was nine, I was not only cooking more advanced dishes, but also baking really cool desserts from scratch and using the kitchen oven by myself. We only had an old cookbook in the house that had been handed down to my mom as a wedding gift—the pages were old and torn, but it had a lot of great recipes. Because we didn't have (and couldn't afford) many of the ingredients, I became very creative with what the cookbook suggested and what we actually had in our cupboards. This was how I learned to adapt recipes.

It's actually pretty easy: Read through several of your favorites, and substitute some of your own ingredients to make your own unique, creative dish. Like the rest of your dance through life, allow this new treat to be your own individual expression. Today, there are plenty of low-fat, low-sugar cookbooks and courses to guide you, and you may or may not want to change a few things. I still adapt dishes with ingredients that I like (all healthy, of course), making them my own. Neena and I have even included some of these favorite recipes of ours for you to try (see page 157). Feel free to play with any of the ingredients to fit the uniqueness in your own creativity.

If you do a lot of your own food prep, there are simple ways to lighten up and change your cooking methods. When preparing foods, stick to steaming, boiling in a small amount of water, or sautéing in extra-virgin coconut oil. Avoid fried foods; instead, bake, broil, poach, or grill. Also, try not to microwave food because this changes the molecular structure, creating substances not known in nature—so who the heck knows what they're doing in your body? Besides, I can usually tell the difference in taste.

If you're a poultry eater, remove the skin before preparing your chicken or turkey, and you can adapt any of your favorite recipes by either using smaller amounts of sugar and fat or preferably substituting them with natural sweeteners and healthy fats. Many traditional ethnic foods are healthy to begin with, and require just a bit of tinkering to fit into your new, lighter menu. A simple way to wake up flavors is to add ethnic herbs and spices to give your food an exotic kick. And remember, good-tasting food doesn't have to be complicated. When you start with fresh, high-quality ingredients, you don't have to do a lot of fancy footwork to bring out their flavors.

So now that you know some basics, why not prepare a healthy, home-cooked meal for your special someone? There's no need to reveal your cooking secrets, the adaptation, or the fact that it's healthy. All he'll know is that it feels good and sensual in his belly. . . .

ON THE ROAD AND ON THE JOB

As we said, you need to be clever in order to make your new menu work for you. Half the time, Neena and I are on the road, and when we travel, we usually call ahead to see what's on the hotel or airline menu and what kinds of restaurants are in the surrounding area. Most of the time, we carry food with us—sometimes one whole suitcase is just full of our favorite dishes! (Nothing beats the love and taste of home cooking!) We also pack our own food when we need to go on a photo shoot or a tour, rather than depending only on the usual catered fare, which may offer foods that we prefer not to eat.

Imagine security staff at the airport when they see packets of dried seaweed; coconut balls; flaxseed crackers; and jars of powdered, dehydrated greens, herbs, and spirulina. If we're stuck in some hotel room in the middle of nowhere, at least we're not doomed to greasy quesadillas! Similarly, if you work in an office, you can bring snacks to work and try to talk your boss into giving you smaller breaks throughout the day so that you can eat your mini-meals. Tell him or her that you'll be much more efficient and productive if you can eat several small meals rather than one big lunch. Ask for a trial period and see if he or she notices a difference. We've done this with our staff, and the whole group says that they feel better and more energetic, and I agree.

EATING OUT

If packing food isn't your thing, eating out at restaurants can be belly-friendly, too. The most basic rule of thumb is to watch your portions. (Remember, you never know when you'll have the urge to get up and dance, so you don't want to be too full!) I know it's tempting, but being in a restaurant is not a license to overeat, even if it's a special occasion. I usually ask how big the portions are; if they're large, Neena and I will split a dish. If you're dining alone or sharing is not an option, box it and take it home or ask for smaller portions. Overeating means paying for the meal twice: once with money and then again with your body! So be bold, speak up, and order exactly what you want ("Make that grilled, please, with the sauce on the side," and "I'd rather not have bread, thanks"). Be polite, but firm—you're in charge!

Here are some strategies to convert specific types of menus to be more belly-friendly:

— **Indian:** A good choice because of the emphasis on vegetables, lentils, and beans. But watch out for dishes that overdo the *ghee* (clarified butter), and dance away from those fried breads dripping with fat. The best bets are tandooris and vegetarian side dishes; if you're confident with spicy food, indulge in masalas and curries. (In India, the herb turmeric is said to be good for Alzheimer's.) Request to lighten any fat or *ghee,* and if you don't like heavy spices, ask for mild curries *without* added dairy. (Many times the chef will add milk or cream to downplay the spices.)

— **Japanese:** Plenty of low-fat/healthy-fat cooking (and noncooking, if you like sashimi or sushi) here. Avoid tempuras and other fried dishes; start with a filling miso soup and a side of sea vegetables; and ask for food to be prepared steamed or poached. Japanese chefs add sugar to many of their dishes, sometimes even in the sushi rice to make it "sticky," so ask for items with no sugar.

— **Mexican:** Another potentially good choice because of the traditional beans and vegetables, but this cuisine can also contain a lot of fat. Many of the foods, especially refried beans, contain lard. The best choices are ceviche, enchiladas, soft tacos, vegetarian burritos, whole (not refried) beans, and fajitas or grilled meats. Ask for no cheese, since most restaurant types are very high in fat, and it's extremely hard to digest melted cheese.

— **French:** Old-style French cooking is rich with creamy, buttery sauces, but nouvelle cuisine is lighter and even tastier, in our opinion. The best bets are anything grilled, steamed, or broiled. If you must order dessert, share it with a few friends.

— **Italian:** Many of the main dishes can be quite fatty, but many appetizers and side dishes are healthy green salads or simply prepared vegetables. Again, grilled meat, poultry, and seafood are your best bets. If you have pasta, choose the primavera and eat one bite of veggies for every forkful of pasta. If you must have pizza, order it with lots of vegetable toppings, and again try to get it without (or with very little) cheese.

— **Chinese:** So many dishes are based on vegetables that you can't go wrong if you can find a place that will prepare them with a minimum of oil. Poached, baked, steamed, clay-pot, and quick-sautéed dishes are the best bets. But pass on the plentiful deep-fried items such as egg rolls and wontons. Stick with vegetables, and if you eat chicken, ask for it to be skinless. Some Chinese restaurants now have brown rice, which is great, but watch out for the sauces, since they may contain sugar and/or preservatives such as MSG.

— **Middle Eastern:** This usually offers lots of good choices, but they serve lots of meats, so watch your portions! Stay away from falafel (which is deep-fried), and stick with tabouli, baba ghanoush, hummus, and salads. We often order a shwarma without the bread! My favorite breakfast item is Egyptian *Ful Madamis,* which is fava beans and lentils with olive oil, lemon juice, and garlic.

— **Thai:** Unfortunately, Thais add lots of sugar to most of their dishes, and many restaurants also tend to use too much oil. Ask for food to be cooked with little oil, or order foods such as fish to be steamed or baked with a side of veggies.

— **Deli:** Choose vegetable salads without oil or mayonnaise-laden dressings and cold cuts without the bread. You could have freshly roasted turkey and chicken, water-packed tuna, or lean roast beef on whole-grain breads, if you must, now and then. If you order a sandwich, and it's one of those supersized monstrosities, only eat half and save the rest for tomorrow, or split it with someone.

— **Fast food:** You don't have to pick what everyone else is eating! Get radical and order a plain burger or grilled chicken without the bun and a salad. Better yet, go to a health-food counter or juice bar and order a shake without added sugar. Now *that's* fast food you can dance on.

Bon Appétit!

So now you have an idea about what works for Neena and me, and a plan that will likely work for you, too. These changes will really add up to a sexier, naturally trimmer belly that's right for your body type. As the weeks and months go by, you'll have more energy, endurance, and confidence that will change your life. Don't hesitate to tweak these steps a little, based on what *your* belly, body, and mind can handle. After all, that's what this book is about! Experiment to see what works for you, and what changes will make this way of eating work even better for your life. Just keep sight of the overall picture: a lighter, more energizing way of eating.

Give yourself time to adjust to these new tastes and proportions. You didn't develop your current eating habits overnight, and they won't change that quickly either. Take small steps and small bites, and you'll be more likely to succeed. Think of it not as depriving yourself of something, but as eating in a new way—almost adopting a whole new culture! Instead of thinking, *I can't have this,* think, *Oh, I want some of that!*

Don't pine for white bread; instead, have some fresh beet salad sprinkled with exotic spices or a celery stick with almond butter. Yum! Rather than concentrating on what's off the menu, open your eyes and mind and think of all the things that *are* on it. You'll get out of your rut and might actually be eating more variety than before . . . and you'll enjoy one of life's greatest pleasures. Like your dance movements, you can be strong, flexible, joyful, and creative in your food choices.

And Don't Forget . . .

Live a little! Enjoy yourself at parties and during holidays. They're special times, and munching carrot sticks and sipping Perrier while everyone else is having chips and margaritas will make you feel deprived. So sample the food, have a drink, watch your portions, and get on the dance floor to work it off!

Don't obsess; just lighten up in your relationship with food. And don't worry about counting the beats in the music or knowing the best time or place to display your hip drops, because the next chapter will teach you how to listen in every way. Now, go on . . . show off your fabulous dancer's body!

Chapter Three

Listen with Your Belly . . . a Fusion of Brains and Beauty
by Neena

Everyone has music in their life. There are sensual sounds that nature provides for us: the wind whispering, birds singing, crickets chirping, and children giggling. And everyone has experienced rhythm—after all, your heartbeat is the most consistent cadence that you hear. Before you even had ears, you listened to your mother's heart as she carried you inside her. Everyone is exposed to this basic beat, and it never leaves you, even if (like Veena and me) you weren't born into a musical family. Our parents weren't musicians or dancers; and they had no instrument, voice, or body training of any sort. Except for singing in the shower and at a few family gatherings, I can't remember them ever creating music or moving to it.

As kids, my sister and I still managed to create a grand effect. We'd sit right in front of the stereo speakers and listen to the music, totally engrossed in the different Indian beats and melodies. We'd even memorize the words, and many times we'd create a whole story from one song. This was our first discovery of learning how to choreograph. First feel the beats, listen to the different instruments, memorize the lyrics next, then identify the central theme of the piece of music . . . and there you have it: A story is told through movement.

Being poor, our parents couldn't afford any dance lessons, so Veena and I didn't know that people actually had formal training in moving their bodies. We never analyzed how to create one dance step and then flow to the next—we just did it without thinking! This was our first encounter with movement through intuition.

Veena was my first audience, fan, and critic, and I was hers. We danced in front of each other, and listened to each other's ideas for new songs or steps. Even though we were very shy girls, dancing was a way of expressing words or feelings with movement. Today, our choreographic decisions are still based on the same issues: *What's in that melody that inspires me to move the way I do?*

Music is everything in dance. Without it, how can you be motivated? Whether it's salsa, hip-hop, or jazz, dance can't survive effectively without that magical sound. This is why we've dedicated an entire chapter to listening: It's the key to helping create choreography, whether you're working out a dance routine or your life. Good planning requires listening to and understanding the music . . . and your inner voice.

Merge with the Music

Many people are drawn to belly dance because of the mesmerizing, soulful music. We'll be showing you specific moves in the next chapter, but for now we want you to start using music to exercise and stretch your brain.

Maybe you're already familiar with Arabic tunes from Internet sources, the radio, or a nearby music store. But if you're not accustomed to listening to this genre, it might feel and sound pretty mysterious, and maybe even a little strange compared to more familiar songs. Eastern and Western music each have their own set of rules and tools—that is, rhythms and sounds. It's like listening to another language.

By the way, "Western" music in this context doesn't refer to country-and-western. I really mean it in the broader sense of what people listen to in most non-Eastern cultures, such as those in Europe and North America. When I say "Arabic," I'm including classical, folk, modern, and pop compositions from Arabic-speaking countries—such as Egypt, Lebanon, Iraq, Jordan, and the regions of North Africa. When I say "Middle Eastern," I'm also including other countries, such as Israel and Iran.

Some of the melodies are fast and daring, while some are slow, sad, or perhaps spiritual; but they're all soulful. On the DVD included with this book, we've given you a sampling of Arabic music with a variety of rhythms, played on many traditional instruments. Each belly-dance movement we teach has its own musical composition, so if you're a newbie, you won't need to look any further. You've got a built-in place to start.

To "listen with your belly" effectively, we recommend that you play the DVD using the "Music Only" selection on the menu so that you're not looking at the images on the screen. That way, it will be easier for you to focus on the music itself and not be distracted by the visual movement. Set aside enough time to play the entire 35-minute program from beginning to end. Even if you've heard this type of music before, try to experience it this time with new appreciation. Allow the sounds to guide and open your senses.

As you listen, you might notice some interesting feelings coming up: The different beats and melodies might make you feel exotic, mysterious, or more lively and feminine. You might feel as though the songs are connecting with another part of you . . . a part that maybe you suspected was there just trying to get out. If you allow it to happen, this can make you soar—lifting and carrying you along, almost like a magic-carpet ride. A friend of mine calls it "merging with the music."

Go on, set the scene by lowering the lights, kicking off your shoes, changing into comfortable clothing, lighting some candles, and maybe even burning some incense or using aromatherapy oils. The most important thing is to just let go and surrender to the sounds.

Neena & Veena's Guide to Belly-Dance Music

Music can be complicated, and you may be wondering *how* you should be approaching this aspect of getting in touch with both your inner and outer belly. Veena and I want you to hear in new ways and at deeper levels than ever before, so we're sharing our guidelines to help you make your way through the forest of sounds. Let's start with the most basic aspect: listening.

LISTENING 101

When I'm listening to music, I like to first do so for pure enjoyment. So to begin, pick one of our songs from the DVD. Close your eyes, and imagine yourself being transported to an ancient magical place. Go ahead: Open all of your senses when listening to music. After hearing it for the first time, how did it make you feel? Now, go back to the same song and listen for the beat. This is usually established by the drums. Let's assume that rhythm is one of the simpler, even ones: 2/4 or 4/4 rhythm that stays consistent (that is, you'll naturally begin to count, tap your foot, or clap: 1-2-3-4, when listening to it).

Now, tap your foot to the beat. What's the tempo: slow, medium, or fast? What other instruments can you hear besides the drums? You may not yet be familiar with their specific names, but you may be able to tell whether the particular instrument is a stringed one (such as a *kanoon,* violin, or *oud*) or a wind instrument (such as a *ney* or *mizmar*). Determine what the chorus or "hook" (a particular phrase that catches your attention) is and identify the verses in the song. How many times do you hear each part? Listening in this way will open up new dimensions in each composition of any kind of music, whether it's Middle Eastern, Latin, or Western.

Moving to the Music

I find music to be the inspiration for Veena's and my choreography. Arabic tunes in particular allow the body to move in feminine, sensual ways. The melodies may suggest certain movements, and the rhythms and tempos may inspire us as far as how to sequence and pace them.

When you follow the movements on the DVD (which we'll teach you in Chapter 4), you may notice that we used lighter, more melodic tunes for many of the upper-body movements; and an earthier, more grounded sound for the lower-body steps. One of our teachers in Egypt used to say, "The lower body expresses the heartbeat [drums]; the upper body expresses the emotion [stringed instruments]." This has been one of the ways in which Veena and I have determined much of our choreography, even when we were little.

But you don't have to be a professional choreographer—or even know any belly-dance steps—to be able to go along with this sexy, joyous, soulful music. So if you feel the urge, go right ahead and start moving, whether you know how to belly dance or not. See what comes out as you allow the music to whisper to your body—that's what Veena and I do. You may use a style that you're familiar with, such as a simple stretch or even a ballet step; or you might find yourself moving in a way that you never have before, creating something that has no label. That's great!

There are no rules, so don't judge yourself . . . just do what you feel like doing. You're just getting to know the music, and freely moving to it is a great way to establish a relationship with it. The sensual feeling and driving beat of Arabic melodies brings you more in touch with your primal, rhythmic self, a more sensual, feminine being. At the very least, it's a great workout, relieves stress, and is fun!

Fine-Tune Your Listening

Once you've taken these liberating steps in listening and movement, you might want to graduate to another level. Go back and listen to the songs on the DVD, but this time, you'll be paying attention to new things. Try to isolate the different instruments and feel the different beats, rhythms, and tempos in each song. As you listen, you'll find that each song may give your belly certain feelings. Much of this is because of the different instrumentations. Listen to how the instruments interact and "play" with each other. The *oud* and the *kanoon*, both stringed instruments, each express different shades of mystical and sensuous feelings. (See the following page for more detailed explanations of these instruments.)

Arabic, Middle Eastern, and Indian music is based on a modal tone system (similar to the notes in a Western scale), but with quarter notes or even microtones (smaller than the quarter step) in between the notes. In Western music, there are 12 notes to a scale. In Middle Eastern music, however, there are up to 24 notes; this is what gives the sound its otherworldly quality. In Arabic music, there are *maqam,* the mysterious melodies that draw the listeners inside themselves, and that can also influence emotions and parts of the body. (In Indian music, there are *ragas,* many of them composed for specific purposes, to evoke specific feelings, to be healing, and to coincide with specific emotions, occasions, or times of the day.)

As I mentioned, Arabic music can be complex, and the rhythms may overlap. Most popular Western music usually has an even rhythm of 4 beats to a measure (4/4), and the quarter note gets one count. Arabic music has a variety of rhythms: Some are even, such as *masmoudi saquire* (known as *belady* in the U.S.; 4/4), *shiftatelli* (slow 8/4 rhythm), and *ayyub* (2/4 rhythm). Others have an uneven tempo, such as *dor hendi* (7/8 rhythm) or the Turkish *karshlama* (9/8 rhythm), which sounds like an extra beat has been thrown in. Many modern and pop Arabic and Indian songs also have even tempos and are easy to follow. I know this is a lot of information, but don't worry—there won't be a quiz!

You might find that you experience music on a deeper level when you understand the details and intricacies of the rhythms, melodies, and instruments. And you may even be the center of attention at the next party or club where they're playing Arabic music: "Oh, I just love this shiftatelli, don't you? It's so soulful! And what about the guy on the oud? He's awesome!"

Need Baby Steps?

Even though Veena and I were born and raised in California, we grew up listening to Indian music at home and at family get-togethers from the time we were infants. As we got a little older, we discovered Middle Eastern music through our relatives who lived in Iran and the Gulf region. I remember when Veena and I were in the fourth grade, our teacher encouraged the students to bring their favorite recordings of artists for show-and-tell. When it was our turn, we brought Middle Eastern and Indian music, of course.

Musical Instruments— Instruments of Desire

These traditional Middle Eastern instruments are still used to make belly-dance music. Oriental keyboards are mostly electronic now, since they can be used to create many different sounds, including traditional ones, such as the accordion.

- **Dumbek:** Also called Egyptian tabla; a drum shaped like an hourglass. This provides the basic rhythm.

- **Oud:** An Arabic instrument with 11 strings, it looks like a guitar with a narrower body and shorter neck. It has a soulful, haunting sound and is the forerunner of the lute.

- **Def:** An Egyptian tambourine that's also used in a manner similar to a drum.

- **Dohla:** A large drum with a bass sound.

41

- **Hi-hats:** Full-size cymbals made of hammered metal.
- **Kanoon:** A Turkish harplike instrument with 72 strings that's played horizontally. (Also spelled "qanun.")
- **Ney:** Traditional flute in Arabic folk and Turkish music.
- **Riqq:** Arabic tambourine.
- **Tabla:** Indian drums.
- **Kemanga:** A violin.
- **Rebaba:** A stringed instrument with one or two strings played with a bow.
- **Mizmar:** A wind instrument.
- **Zills:** Also called "sagat" or finger cymbals, these are four small brass discs played by either the belly dancer or a musician; they produce a bell-like sound.

It was interesting to observe how the other kids seemed confused at first: They couldn't sing along because they didn't know the foreign words, and they weren't sure how to dance to it—but they sure felt the beat! They moved however they wanted, and to me, that's all that mattered.

So East met West . . . halfway at least (this was our first introduction to dance fusion, actually). Eventually, Veena and I grew to love all types of Western music, too. We enjoyed modern classics such as Frank Sinatra and Nat King Cole, and there was even a time when we were obsessed with '60s and '70s retro-Western-pop music . . . the clothes, the makeup, and the whole outrageous feel. All in all, Veena and I love just about every kind of Western music—including hip-hop, R & B, rock, and even country.

If you've tried listening to our DVD and found that you're not quite ready to surrender to the Eastern beat, give it some time. You might want to start with a close examination of some music that you *are* more familiar with, such as contemporary rock, rhythm and blues, oldies, soulful love songs, or whatever. Try listening to that with your belly and see where it takes you. Then you might take the next step and go on to some fusion, world-beat-type music. Fusion style is like a tasty music recipe because it can blend anything: Western with Eastern music, Eastern with Latin, and contemporary with ancient sounds. Anything goes!

Fusion in the Arabic and Indian music world is nothing new. Those composers have always shared ideas and instrumentations with other styles and cultures. Some Western pop and rock artists have incorporated Middle Eastern vocals and instruments into their music. Amr Diab, a famous Egyptian singer, has also incorporated some other world music into some of his CDs—what an awesome combo!

Bollywood (a form of Indian pop music from films) got its name by fusing "Hollywood" with "Bombay." For the last 50 years, Indian pop music has been incorporating other cultural music, including Arabic, Asian, as well as Western, and it's recently fused with R & B and hip-hop. In India, this is known as "music masala." (*Masala* means "mixture," derived from *garam masala,* a common food spice found in every Indian kitchen.)

Arabic music has also recently become more Westernized, making it more appealing to Americans as well as to the younger generations in Egypt and other Arabic-speaking countries. The pop music is fun, and it has a new, fresh vibe. Of course, we'll always have a place in our hearts for the classic songs such as "Aziza," "Leylet Hob," "Alf Leyla Wa Leyla," or "Zeina." Veena and I love fusion, and we're happy to see that so many people are into it. It's a great way to introduce other cultures to each other. World beat and global music are in the air all over the world. It's a very exciting time in music—and it's here to stay.

Best of all, these styles are all danceable, whether you're in a club, a class, or the privacy of your own home. In some belly-dance classes in the U.S., teachers are playing Arabic pop or even techno and adapting traditional movements to it, giving belly dance a whole different feel . . . we call it "dance fusion."

Over the years, Veena and I have belly danced in many Western music videos for famous artists. So why not belly dance to hip-hop, rhythm and blues, or pop? If you're in tune with your own creativity, we feel that there's nothing wrong with adding a Western move here and there. We're not purists, because the dance isn't.

Where to Find Belly-Dance Music

These days, it's pretty easy to find Middle Eastern music, and these recommendations will get you started. There are Internet sites such as **www.radiobastet.com**, which plays vintage belly-dance music from the 1950's; and AOL Radio, which has several stations that include this genre. Visit a music store and sample the albums at their listening posts (go to the World Music section). And you may even find Middle Eastern or Indian radio stations in your area.

Some of the Top Arabic Artists

These are some of our favorite singers, whose music we play in our classes:

- Hakim
- Hisham Abbas
- Amir Ragheb
- Diana Hadad
- Ragheb Alama
- Mustafa Amar
- Warda
- Setrak Sarkissian
- Mohammed Abdel Wahab

Of course, there are many, many more!

This art form has evolved over the centuries with the changing times, different locales, and shifts in women's place in the world. It should and will continue to evolve.

So, once you're comfortable with fusion style—go for it! Move on from that genre and immerse yourself in all aspects of belly-dance music. Give yourself a musical makeover, as we did.

Listen to Your Belly: Your Sixth Sense

I've found that being in tune with, or listening to, my belly gives me freedom while creating choreography. I don't think about the next step, I just move—that is, I allow my belly to move me. When Veena and I perform together, we have to be so in tune with one another that even our improvisation looks like we've rehearsed it for a long time. A lot of Western jazz artists also do this when playing; and the next time they perform the same music, it will sound completely different. It's the same concept in belly dance: It may be different every time you perform.

Your choreography may change with your mood, your audience, and your environment, but you have to be in tune with your belly. One of our musician friends used to say that when he plays a solo *taksim*, which is improvisational music, he allows his belly to move his fingers to create a "dance" on his oud.

Beyond inspiring people to dance, we've discovered that listening to music with your belly—that is, with your soul—can affect your brain, your body, and even your whole life. It can help you become more in tune with yourself, make your life feel more rhythmic, more in sync with your surroundings, more flowing, and simply "right." Opening your ears and your belly to exotic sounds from the Middle East, in particular, can open up fresh options for hearing and seeing everything. Most exciting of all, it can lead to new ways of tapping in to your innate intuition in order to make smart decisions in your life, from picking the right shade of lipstick to finding your soul mate.

So far you've been practicing how to listen *with* your belly, to get beyond your ears and brain and really feel the rhythm and melody of the music in your center. Becoming familiar with Arabic music is a fun way to get you in the belly-dance groove. When you open up and expose yourself to a feast of sounds, something amazing happens: You also get more in tune with yourself and other people. That's because listening and dancing to music allows you to express who you are.

The music itself triggers creativity in your mind, and by getting yourself up and moving, it gets your creative energy flowing. As a result, you're accessing the parts of your brain that trigger your intuitive ability, because these both come from the right side of the brain. Getting lost in this music and merging with it may also get your mind off a stressful day, especially when the sound is fresh and unfamiliar. If it holds no memories for you, then it frees you to think new thoughts. Taksim, in particular, is calming and relaxing, allowing your intuition to emerge because the centering qualities help you focus.

We think of intuition as "listening *to* your belly" because it's as if you're tuning in to your own *inner* music. Intuition is sometimes referred to as "gut feelings," your "sixth sense," or "vibes." In my mind, they're all the same thing: They tell you what you really feel, know, need, and want. Listening to your belly doesn't mean being ruled by your heart (or your appetite or hormones). The fact is, its outcome can be the opposite. You see, listening to your heart is acting based on how you're feeling emotionally, but when listening to your belly, you'll make your decision while centering yourself without letting the emotions get in the way.

Some choices (such as deciding between a salad or brown rice or watching this movie or that one) you can make in a snap, and there's no harm done if you're wrong. Other decisions (such as getting married, buying a house, or hiring a plastic surgeon) require research and take time. Let your intuition be your guide.

Before you act, you need to gather and digest information. I remember that our aunt used to always say, "Whatever happens, it's God's will" (in the Urdu and Arabic languages, we say *inshallah*). But there's a fine line between fatalism—sitting around and waiting for something to happen—and being able to discern when the timing is or isn't right. In our early career, Veena and I didn't hang out waiting for the phone to ring for our next job. We got out there and created our own path and destiny. But we always relied on our bellies to guide us on financial, personal, and even creative decisions, as well as which jobs to accept and which to turn down . . . the list goes on and on.

Just as music inspires and influences our dance choreography, our inner-belly music guides us in making decisions in life. Veena and I believe that it's important for everyone to enhance their intuitive abilities. People have choices every day, and sometimes they find themselves making stupid decisions, no matter how smart they are. If the phrase "What was I thinking?" is all too familiar to you, maybe your intuitive motor could use just a little tune-up. Whether you're trying to decide about your hair color, your clothes, your husband, your job, your shoes, or your lunch, intuition helps you take the next big and little steps in life.

Listening internally helps you make the right decisions for yourself. It's not being selfish to take care of yourself and do what you need to do— whether that means making the time to take belly-dance classes, experimenting with new makeup, or switching careers.

TRUSTING YOUR INNER VOICE

When my sister and I were about five years old, we heard the doctors telling our bedridden mom to stay put. Our belly feelings, however, were telling us that gentle movement would ease her rheumatoid arthritis. And it was true: We noticed that whenever she was able to get up and move, her body responded well, and she felt better. Our gut feelings were right on target, and today, doctors usually recommend that their arthritis patients stay active!

As adults, we use our own intuition all the time to guide us professionally and socially. Our bellies help us decide what projects to work on, which friends to hang out with, the best foods for us to eat, even what movie to see. Against all odds, our bellies guided Veena and me toward our careers in the first place. And they continue to steer us to positive situations and protect us from the negative. I can't tell you how often we've been offered terrific-sounding jobs and tours with certain artists that just didn't feel right, whether it was because of timing or a situation. Had we ignored our gut feelings and gone against the grain, we wouldn't have gotten other opportunities that were more suitable for our lifestyle. I hear of so many similar situations with my friends and family.

Generally, kids are great at listening to their bellies, and they'll just tell you honestly what they like or don't like and whom they trust or mistrust. Unfortunately, as adults, their brains take over, and they quit listening to themselves and to others. So if you're making one poor choice after another, if you have a hard time making decisions and wait too long to take action, or if you haven't been trusting your gut instincts, then it's time for a change. Through this book you can learn to listen to your belly, trust it, and learn to hear others even more.

FINE-TUNE YOUR INTUITION

Veena and I have learned to fine-tune our sixth sense by listening to our bellies, and you can, too! We firmly believe that everyone has this capability in some form or another to a certain degree; they just need to learn how to tune in. The first thing to do is to start believing that gut feelings are real and of value.

Some time ago, "woman's intuition" was a sexist joke or considered to be old-fashioned superstition. Today we've come full circle: Many scientists acknowledge that there's something to it, and they know that dismissing this sixth sense is passé. I believe that these powers will continue to get more recognition in all fields. After all, police departments and company CEOs are already hiring intuitives or psychics to help them solve crimes and make business decisions. It's quite thrilling to acknowledge the value of woman's intuition as a component of your own intelligence, so be proud of it, just as you're satisfied with your curves. Accentuate it, use it, and don't let it be squashed by other people. Veena and I have rarely had a situation where our instincts were wrong. Sure, we've made mistakes, but it was always because we weren't listening to our vibes, and we let our hearts influence us instead of our belly feelings.

Next, realize that a sixth sense comes in many forms. I'm an intuitive person, and one way that I get information is through handwriting analysis. Veena's particular skill is dream analysis—that's her way of receiving messages. *Your* intuition can be something that you feel, something that you see, or both. Sometimes a woman's gut feeling might be based on heightened senses; for example, a mother can know that her child is in need because she's "heard" a whimper that's inaudible to everyone else.

Your other senses can even get in the way of your sixth sense! They can actually distract you from what's really going on, or you'll read too much into them. For example, when you meet someone for the first time, your belly can give you information about a person within the first five seconds. Don't try to second-guess your first instinct—you could end up changing your feelings, and even talk yourself into thinking differently about that person. Stay with that first gut feeling you got the moment you saw him or her: thumbs up or thumbs down? Is this a con artist or someone who really has your best interests at heart?

Acknowledge that initial gut feeling and make a note of how it feels. For me, when something doesn't feel right, I get a twist or pull in my belly. For you, it might be a heavy feeling, a sound like bees buzzing, a little surge of energy, a tugging, an alarm going off, or something else entirely different. (When something feels right to me, however, it just feels good, like sunshine in a meadow.) Then the next time you meet that person, use your senses to gather information and compare it to your initial flash. This is one way of putting your intuition to the test to see if it's right.

Another way to access your intuition is to pay attention to signs in your environment. For example, I was having a meeting with someone in a restaurant, trying to decide if I should do business with him. At that point, another man walked in the front door of the restaurant carrying a big ladder. *How unusual,* I thought. *Guys with ladders usually enter through the service entrance at the back. Why is he coming through here, now?* When I saw that out-of-place ladder, I interpreted that as a climbing-up opportunity—a good sign.

A lot of messages are given to us when we don't even expect them. One time Veena and I were on our way to a gig, and on the flight, she ended up sitting next to a wonderfully sweet 80-year-old woman who told her out of the blue, "Luxembourg is so nice this time of year." I found that odd, because we were contemplating whether to take a job in Luxembourg! So we decided to go for it after all, and we had a great time. In India and the Middle East, it's said that God gives us signs in ways that we, as common people, will understand.

Whenever I encounter a new situation or person, I wonder, *If my belly could talk, what would she say?* "What a caring person!" "I don't trust this person for business!" "This man isn't right for you!" In the end, my belly is always right. I've always regretted when my brain talks me out of what my belly is telling me, saying things such as, "C'mon, hurry up, you've got to decide . . . everyone is recommending this company . . . the price is really cheap . . . "

Our advice is to acknowledge the feeling in your belly when you believe that your intuition is working. Our great-grandmother, who lived to be 104 years old, said that denying your God-given intuitive gift is unhealthy. If you're "holding in" your emotions and not allowing your inner belly to express itself, then your body potentially can suffer with weight gain and health problems. She always believed that good health and beauty came from the belly.

BELLY TALK

Allowing your intuition to develop can help you communicate and be on the same wavelength with other people. This is especially effective if the other person is also open to intuitive communica-

Belly Tip: Set Aside Time

Set aside time each day—in the morning just before or after you get up, or at night before you go to sleep—to take a moment to listen to your belly. Close your eyes to shut out distractions, and become aware of how this part of you feels and what it's telling you. Some specific questions may pop up; if so, make note of them. Pay particular attention during times of stress or when you need to make an important decision.

49

Eat Intuition-Supporting Foods

It's so much easier to pay attention to intuitive feelings if your belly isn't all weighed down with heavy food. When you eat lighter, purer foods (such as those we recommend in Chapter 2 and the Appendix), it gives your mind the space to be creative and more intuitive. In India, my uncle used to say that eating lighter foods such as fruits, vegetables, whole grains, and nuts (which are called *sattvic* foods) calms and clarifies the mind, as well as the body.

Belly Voice

While we're on the subject of listening, have you heard yourself talk lately? Is it the kind of voice you'd want to hear? Do you sound happy, tired, or even a little whiny? To find out, grab the video that you made in Chapter 1 and take a moment to listen to yourself again, focusing on the sounds rather than the content of what you said. If you didn't make a videotape then, go ahead and make an audio recording now. If you don't love what you hear and decide that your voice needs a sensual makeover, try this exercise that Veena and I learned while studying classical singing. It's also a great tune-up for public speakers and actors!

Begin by either standing or sitting in a comfortable position. Let's make that sure you're breathing correctly, because if your breathing is shallow, so is your voice. A shallow, thin sound lacks confidence, and it can come across as either old and weak or young and insecure. Your voice will never resonate properly and live up to its true potential without the power of your lungs behind it.

Breathe deeply through your nose, sending the air into your belly starting from your lower abdomen and lower back, then filling your upper belly, and finally expanding your rib cage to its full extent. Then exhale, bringing in your lower abs toward your spine. Complete five full breaths. The sixth time, try humming as you exhale, keeping your forehead, brows, and jaw relaxed.

Keep a soft "inner smile" as you hum—that is, feel as if you're smiling, uplifted, and happy. Try different pitches, starting at a comfortable lower range and humming your way up higher. You should feel a nice little buzzing vibration going from your chest to your lips, and up to your forehead. (Make sure that you keep your lips lightly pressed together.)

By practicing these simple breathing and humming exercises, your voice will become sensual, caressing, and confident in no time at all. These techniques keep your vocal chords light, airy, and "off the throat," which will get rid of the crackles in your voice and make you sound 10 or even 20 years younger!

tion—it takes two to tango! Whenever Veena and I perform our dance numbers, we allow our bellies to listen and communicate to each other . . . and to the audience. We work on being "in tune."

As I mentioned, I often imagine what my belly might say about a situation. Veena and I have been doing this for a long time. I remember that when we were little, we used to have a game where we'd lift our shirts up, exposing our bellies, and imagine that they'd talk to each other. We'd pretend that our little belly buttons were mouths, drawing little ears on either side of them and little eyes above. We'd jiggle and manipulate our midsections, and create fun voices for each character.

You might think that it was just a funny childhood game, except that as an adult, whenever I perform on stage, film, or television as an actress, I still imagine my belly with ears listening and talking through the navel to the actor performing with me. By doing this, my emotions connect to the other person, which improves my acting.

Veena told me about an acting student of hers who used this technique in his personal life. As he applied "belly talking," his days of interrupting people in the middle of a conversation dwindled more and more. He started listening to his wife more and really heard what she was saying—and their marriage danced for joy!

A New Way of Listening, a New Way to Dance

Giving your music collection a makeover is a painless confirmation that change can be a good thing. By opening up your "belly ears" to new beats, sounds, and melodies, you'll open up all of yourself to new possibilities, including fresh ways of moving, thinking, and feeling. Hearing new sounds and enjoying creative movement help you let go of old ideas and entrenched ways of doing things so that you can dance toward something new.

Now that you've discovered a new way of listening, it will be easier to explore what else is out there for you. What has your sight, smell, touch, and taste been missing? And while you're exploring new territory, you can use your intuition to make good choices by listening to what your "inner belly" is saying.

When you're dancing, something inside tells you what your next step is—what direction to go in. This type of creative intuition works in life, too. Should I do a turn, a dip, a side step, or a step forward or backward? Should I travel or stay in one place? Intuition will help you be a more sensitive and confident decision maker, whether you're playing the role of dancer, friend, mother, company vice president, or lover. Use this gift to choreograph your new life!

And now that you've got a feel for the music—let's give you more details about the movements. . . .

✳ ✳ ✳　✳ ✳ ✳

Chapter Four

Shape Up Your Belly . . .
the Ultimate Workout
by Veena

Neena and I love belly dance because it's an amazing, sensual workout for the female body. Like other forms of physical activity, it shapes, tones, and makes us feel good mentally and physically. But belly dance is so much more than that: It's a complete inner *and* outer beauty workout. Its not only about getting your heart rate up—it's about *movement,* and encompasses all of its aspects: posture, grace, coordination, confidence, fluidity, body awareness, and skill. Yes, belly dance will transform your shape, but it will also change how you move in general and your attitude about your physical self. So if you only want to build muscle, go to the gym and pick up some weights. But if you want the freedom to express yourself, experiment, break out of the traditional-exercise mode, awaken your sensuality, and feel and look feminine . . . then pick up a belly-dance veil!

The Belly and Beyond

When Neena and I taught classes regularly, I noticed that a lot of our students were toning up and losing weight. When a national television show was doing a fitness segment on Neena and me, they came to one of our classes and taped different responses from our students. One of the most typical comments was: "Belly dance is so much fun that it doesn't even feel like I'm working out."

Not surprisingly, this is a superb method of weight control, and often works when other approaches fail. Take, for example, one of my students who'd lost more than 40 pounds in two years through a program of walking and sensible eating, before reaching a stubborn plateau. No matter how she tried, she couldn't make a dent in the remaining 25 pounds that were keeping her from her goal weight. Yet only seven weeks after she added belly dance to her regimen, her weight started dropping again. She told me, "Belly dance has kick-started my metabolism, and I feel great. I'm hooked!"

Another student described herself as a "young but heavy girl" who had the spirit and desire to dance, but whose energy was "sometimes lagging due to [her] weight." She found conventional workouts uncomfortable and too painful to maintain—yet she was amazed that even though she perspired freely during belly-dance sessions, afterward she felt energetic and wasn't in any pain. She began dancing every other day and was happy to say, "Believe it or not, my husband noticed that my weight was dropping. I was so jazzed about the whole thing—I felt stronger, improved my posture, and was looking better. Plus, those sensual movements added some spice to our love life!"

Belly dance works wonders because it's low impact and low intensity, so you can keep going for a longer period of time than with other, more jarring aerobic activities. And it's lots of fun, so you'll *want* to do it longer than other exercises. Plus, this discipline gets you working muscles that you never knew you had, and using them in several new ways.

First, when you perform belly-dance movements correctly, they work specific muscle groups, which means that you train each section more intensely. You isolate your upper and lower body both vertically and horizontally, extending and contracting your muscles in unique ways.

Belly dance really works the core muscles in your abdomen, pelvis, trunk, and back, even though your hips actually "lead" the movements. The steps aren't jarring or invasive; in fact, they feel natural. The circular movements emphasize the curvaceousness of the female body.

All of this adds up to a total-body workout that burns fat gently, safely, and steadily, strengthening your heart and lungs while trimming your thighs, firming up your fanny, and sculpting your arms—in addition to beautifying your tummy! Belly dance is simultaneously modern, ancient, and hip, and it puts you in touch with the sexy siren inside of you.

Although the movements are quite simple and easy to learn, they can be combined into an infinite number of routines that allow you to steadily improve your skills and strut your stuff, whether in your own home, in a class, or in front of an audience. And don't worry if you do sweat—"glowing" is very sensual!

Kama Belly: Sex the Belly Way

Belly dance improves your sex life. Yeah! As you're dancing, those "feel-good" endorphins are released in your brain, making you happier and feeling feminine. Not only will it put you in that "ooooh soooo sexy" mood, but it's a fantastic way of practicing many moves that will come in handy later on—if you know what I mean!

But let's get down to the nuts and bolts, ladies. First, this art form tones the muscles of your inner thighs, derriere, and around your breasts, as well as increasing your stamina. Belly dance is an incredible tension reliever, energy booster, and self-esteem builder. But the outer muscles aren't the only ones working: As you dance, blood goes to your sexual organs, specifically working on the tone of your pelvic region. What's more, the inner vaginal muscles will increase in strength and tightness so that you'll have easier and better orgasms (because you'll have more sensitivity). And after childbirth, your muscles will regain strength more quickly.

Just think: You'll have more sexual confidence and better control in bed! In fact, one of the theories of the origins of belly dance is that experienced women used these dance movements to teach other women how to be good lovers, as well as how to move in order to make childbirth easier. These days, my sister and I find that most women in our classes want to add playfulness and sensuality to their relationships. They're looking for something new and different to surprise and entice their significant others.

Although we've seen many love-life transformations over the years, perhaps the most enjoyable was one that recently took place in front of millions of TV viewers. Neena and I were featured guests on a show that enlisted us to teach a young woman named Dawn how to belly dance to delight her boyfriend. After a few short lessons, the results were taped at a Moroccan restaurant.

Dawn and her unsuspecting sweetie were having dinner, and soon after they arrived, she excused herself to go to the restroom. She quickly changed into a belly-dance costume, and Arabic music began to play. The look on her boyfriend's face when she reappeared and started to perform was absolutely priceless. And when she used her veil seductively to tease him and bring him literally closer to her, he went nuts!

Later Dawn admitted, "I didn't think that I had the femininity to perform the movements, but while I danced, I really felt like a woman. Belly dance gave me the confidence and inner strength I needed to express the seductiveness I'd always wanted to show my boyfriend but didn't know how." Her efforts brought them closer as a couple because he was so touched and pleased.

Dawn's situation isn't unusual: Neena and I have gotten many letters from men, believe it or not. One happy guy wrote: "Thank you! Because of your belly-dance videos, my marriage was saved." He explained that his wife had gained the confidence to become a better lover, so their sex life improved. We hear it all the time from husbands and boyfriends: Learning the sensual moves can help women become more comfortable and proud of their own bodies.

In addition, women tell us that belly dance has helped them before and after giving birth. "My baby girl just popped right out after belly dancing throughout my pregnancy!" one woman confided. Another confirmed that through belly dance, she got back in shape after her son was born—and back in touch with her sexuality. (It's not just us: Physicians have confirmed these benefits.)

Because it's so much fun and so satisfying . . . because it's a total workout that involves all of you: body, mind, spirit, and creativity . . . because the music is so good . . . because you may never know how much more sensual you can become . . . for all of these reasons and more, belly dance is a unique workout that you'll look forward to again and again.

Belly Posture

Before we dive into specific steps, I want to teach what I believe is the foundation of all movements: posture. Beautiful motion begins with proper alignment, whether it's belly dancing in a nightclub or just walking in the park. Without it, everything looks "off" and will lack elegance. A good stance exudes beauty, confidence, poise, power, success, and control; bad posture shows low self-esteem, fear, carelessness, sadness, and even anger. So think of me as your personal-attitude trainer, bringing out the gorgeous, confident woman in you!

First, stand in front of a full-length mirror with your feet parallel and together. Beginning from your head, level your chin so that it's parallel to the floor. If your head is protruding forward (as is often the case), slide your neck back—but not all the way so that you're creating a double chin. Now look at your neck: Is it elongated like a swan's? Check out your shoulders to see if they're even. Make sure that they aren't shrugging up or curving forward—instead, bring them down and away from your ears.

As you look toward your belly, be sure that your rib cage is pulled straight, not splayed out. Arms and fingers should be relaxed by your sides. Keep all of your fingers elegantly closed, slightly fanning out the index and pinky fingers.

Now, level your hips by dropping your tailbone. Your lower belly will automatically slightly lift, and the front of your hips should stay flat (perpendicular to the floor). Try not to collapse, tilt, or bend at the hips, as this changes the look of traditional dance and loses the beauty of the alignment. Keep your knees soft, with your feet firmly planted on the ground from your heels to the tips of your toes.

BELLY POSE

On the DVD, you'll notice that Neena and I start and end each section with we call the "belly pose." This is because some of the movements are based from this pose (such as hip drops and dropkicks, along with a few others), but also because it's elegant and emphasizes the good posture that you just learned.

Let's begin by standing up straight with your feet parallel. Slide one foot directly back just past your heel, and turn out that back foot about 45 degrees for balance. Keep your inner thighs together.

Next, lift your front foot to either a *demi* point (on the ball of the foot) or a full point (on your toes with an arched foot), depending on the move, while keeping that front toe in contact with the floor. Align your ankles directly above your toes, trying not to collapse your ankles outward. For a more elegant line, you can bring your ankle slightly inward toward the opposite foot.

Keep breathing naturally. The upper body should lift up toward the sky, and the lower torso naturally expands down toward the earth. Try this pose in front of a mirror: You embody poise, confidence, and power—and you look beautiful!

Walk Like an Egyptian: Belly Walk

The way a woman walks says so much about her. Her level of awareness, confidence, and even her health and emotional well-being show in the way she walks. As private coaches, we've seen time and time again how women don't realize what they present to the public just by walking.

I tested this with one of my new students. I asked her to walk in front of me in the manner that she normally walks. Her shoulders tended to protrude forward, and her chest caved in. She also had what Neena and I call the "iron walk." You could not only *hear* her heavy footsteps, but also *feel* the vibration from her walk.

Then I told her to apply the Belly Posture to the way she walks. She looked much better than she'd ever imagined. After applying our belly-dance techniques, including a few of the travel steps, her iron walk soon turned to a light feather.

In workshops or classes, when Neena and I have taught choreography to young dancers or newbies, we find that they often look down on the floor as they watch themselves dance. We'll say to them: "Look at your audience, not your feet—the choreography isn't written on the floor!" Whether you're dancing or walking, the same rule applies.

As your private trainer, I'd like you to review the videotape that Neena suggested you use on yourself from Chapter 1. Go through this Belly Posture checklist:

1. Feet parallel
2. Slide chin back
3. Elongate neck
4. Shoulders down and even
5. Close rib cage
6. Relax arms and fingers
7. Drop tailbone

Now I'm going to add a couple of extra rules:

1. Watch and listen for the iron walk.
2. Look ahead and not at the floor.

Good! Now try walking. It may take a little practice to remember everything, but it will become second nature to you.

Oh, and one more thing: Once you practice on our DVD with belly-dance techniques, you'll walk so gracefully! No more "irons" here—save that for your clothes!

The Neena & Veena Belly-Dance Workout

In all of our classes, I've found that my students learned most effectively through repetitions of the same movement. This was how Neena and I created our extremely popular worldwide *Bellydance Fitness for Beginners* series, which gives you a great workout while you're learning how to belly dance.

In this chapter, you'll learn some of our favorite belly-dance movements done in an exercise fashion. Although they're many of the same ones that are on the DVD accompanying this book, we'll be teaching you how to do these steps as a workout, while the video is geared more toward perfecting individual techniques. In addition, this book lets you have it all at your fingertips when a DVD player isn't available.

There are many belly-dance movements and variations. We've chosen these particular ones because they're basic and effective. Physically, they'll improve your muscle tone and increase your flexibility; while emotionally, the healing rhythms will massage away tension, rejuvenating life and energy.

In this workout, we'll show you how to do these steps as a sequence of repetitions (explained below). The DVD shows you the movements, and also teaches you a routine that's an example of one way to put it all together in a fluid, sensual dance. Once you've learned our choreography, don't be shy about creating your own and expressing the unique belly-dance spirit in you.

How to Do the Workout

Now that you've familiarized yourself with rhythms and basic Arabic music thanks to Chapter 3, you may want to try the exercises while playing our DVD with the "Music Only" selection on the menu. If you prefer your own music, that's fine, too—use anything that inspires you. And even if you don't have music, it's not a problem. We're just trying to get your body moving!

Except for the warm-up, which stays the same, this program is progressive: Every time you do it, you'll increase the duration of each movement. The first time you do the workout, repeat each movement for 30 seconds; the next time through, add about 10 more seconds to each step. Keep adding ten seconds per movement each session until you reach your personal goal. To focus properly, we recommend that you spend half the time doing each step slowly (two music beats per movement) and the other half of the time up to tempo (one beat per movement).

For a quick, overall-body workout, I try to get in around eight to ten dance moves within 30 minutes. To work on target zones, I usually focus on five or six steps: I'll pick one and repeat it for an entire song, then when that music ends, I'll go on to the next movement with a new song, and so on. For a lengthier workout—if I want more toning or to burn more fat, for example—I simply repeat the entire 30-minute sequence from start to finish so that I'm dancing for about an hour.

My sister and I have received e-mails from women who said that they liked using our fitness tapes or DVDs twice in a row without stopping because they're having so much fun, and it gives them a longer workout. Others have said that they'll complete two (or even three) different programs of ours back to back—yet whatever you're comfortable with is fine—remember, you're learning to listen to *your* body.

Are you ready to give it a try? Let's sweat to some ancient moves. Here's your cue: and a-one-and-a-two . . .

BELLY WARM-UP

— **Floating arms:** Take a deep inhalation as you raise both arms in front of you, crossing them at the wrists and bringing them overhead. Then allow them to float down to your sides as you exhale. Repeat twice. (I like ending a workout with this one, too.)

— **Neck rolls:** Drop your head to the front, then gently allow it to roll it to one side, releasing any tension. Then let it roll back down and around to the other side. Repeat each side four times. This releases neck tension and opens up your fifth chakra, which relates to communication and creativity.

— **Shoulder rolls:** Roll both shoulders for-   ward, up, back, and around to the starting position; repeat four times. Next, alternate rolling your left and right shoulders, repeating four times on each side. As you move each shoulder around, allow your breath to naturally flow and release into your third and fourth chakras (the power and heart chakras), bringing you feminine empowerment, as well as peace and compassion.

— **Head slide:** Move (but don't tilt) your head from side to side, toward one shoulder and then back to the other, as if you're a village woman balancing a water jug on your head. Keep your upper body tension-free, and think of leading with your ears, while your chin is floating across an imaginary tabletop. This classic belly-dance movement accentuates your neck . . . and it looks exquisite behind a veil!

— **Hip slides:** Check to make sure that your tailbone is dropped; then open your upper body and align your spine as you slide your hips from side to side. Be sure to keep everything up top as still as possible in order to isolate the movement; your legs stay straight as your hips alternate. With each slide, imagine your breath extending outward beyond the sides of your hips, allowing your first and second chakras to open, which will bring you health and dynamic presence, as well as fluidity and grace.

BELLY UPPER-BODY WORKOUT

— **Shoulder shimmy:** This creates excitement and energy in Arabic dance. With your arms extended at shoulder level out to either side and elbows softly bent, alternate pushing each shoulder forward and back. Pretend that each one is a fist and that you're punching one forward as the opposite shoulder punches back. Alternate your shoulders in a slow, steady movement while staying relaxed and trying to keep your arms in place. As you alternate faster, emphasize each one punching forward.

The fastest speed is the actual shimmy, where the shoulders alternate so fast that they almost vibrate. As the name states, these movements come from the shoulders, *not* the chest. This step is typical of the Egyptian style.

— **Snake arms:** Create this by lifting and dropping one elbow. Simply raise your elbow, allowing your wrist and fingers to follow. Then as you drop the elbow, your wrist and fingers follow once again, making a soft, fluid movement. Repeat with the other arm.

— **Snake arms (alternating):** Alternate the arms with one elbow rising up as the other descends. First the elbow goes up (or down), and then the wrist and fingers follow. Elbow, wrist, fingers. This can be done alone or with a veil: Ooooh . . . sssssensual!

BELLY LOWER-BODY WORKOUT

The legs are said to be like the pillars in a temple, representing strength and balance in your lower body. The following movements all help tone and firm your legs, your abdominal muscles, your hips, and your buns.

— **Half hip circles:** Bring your feet into a parallel position. Keeping your belly posture and alignment (see page 56), simply create half circles with your hips: Start from the front and go to the side, then swoop it around to the other side. Pretend that there are two dots displayed at the side of your hips, and that your hips are connecting the dots in a smooth arc. Do this in one direction and then the other.

— **Hip circles:** Now make full, smooth circles. Shift your weight forward, to the side, back, and to the other side, bending the opposite knee as you shift your weight. Imagine drawing a circle on the floor with your hips as you keep your legs together and your knees softly bent. (Notice how free your spine feels.) Your upper body should remain still with your abdominal muscles lifted. Keep your shoulders down and relaxed. Each time you circle your hips to the side, the outside leg bends and your inside leg is straight. Now go the other direction: front, back, front, and back. Repeat, alternating directions.

— **Hip circle and a half:** Put the two preceding movements together to make one full circle plus a half circle, first in one direction and then the other way. Repeat, alternating directions.

— **Adding Travel:** This is a little preview of the category of traveling steps (see page 62), but the focus is really on the hip action. There are four parts to this movement: (1) Step out to the side with your right foot as your hip arcs forward, creating a half circle from left to right; (2) step together with your left foot as you complete the circle arcing backward from the right to the left side; (3) step out with your right foot again and create another front half circle; and (4) bring your left foot in next to the right, ending either with a pointed toe or on a *demi* point (the ball of the foot) so that your left foot is free to go the other way.

You're creating a circle and a half with your hips, while traveling side to side with your feet. The left side goes like this: Step out with the left foot, step in with the right, step out with the left foot, and touch with the right—at the same time that you're creating one and a half circles. Be sure to keep your hips swirling! Repeat, alternating each direction.

— **Big hip circles:** For this one, step your feet out to a wide stance, feet parallel, and simply create a big circle with your hips: Circle forward, side, back, side; then go the other way. As you come around back, keep your belly tucked in. This move is usually accompanied by arms crossed in front of your chest as the hips circle to the back.

— **Hip drops:** This is one of the most common lower-body movements. Begin with your right foot in front of the left with your back knee slightly bent. Point your right toes, lightly touching the floor. Lift your right hip by contracting your side abdominal muscle, and then drop the hip by pushing it down. Contract to lift, and push to drop, keeping your weight on your supporting leg. Make sure that your chest stays high and lifted, and don't bend or collapse in the hips. Pretend that your hip is a hammer, pounding on a nail. Use your front leg for balance as you lift and drop the hip, and keep your inner thighs close together; then work your left side.

— **Hip drop-kicks:** For the drop-kicks, begin with two hip drops, but on the second one, simply straighten your working leg as your foot brushes slightly off the ground: Hip drop, hip drop with a kick. (Don't forget to keep your inner thighs together.) Depending on the music, some dancers like to put a slight bounce in their knees, and leaning back adds some fun. Practice both sides.

— **Hip bumps:** Start with your feet parallel, hip-width apart. Shift your weight to the right side, slightly bending that knee. Now quickly straighten the knee as you squeeze the right glute. Other side. Practice alternating both sides.

— **Hip shimmy:** Don't be nervous about this one. It's easier than it looks—and once you get it, you'll be having so much fun that you won't want to stop! To begin, slowly alternate the legs by bending and straightening each knee, but never locking them. Keep your knees relaxed and your upper body still, as if it was separated from your lower body. Then gradually speed up the tempo, double-time it . . . and finally hit high speed, going as fast as you can. As you increase to this level, I find that tightening the glutes helps the shimmies stay consistent. Keep both heels on the ground, and make a steady rhythm with your knees. If you lose the rhythm, slow down your shimmy and then build back up to speed.

These moves take practice, but once you've learned them, they're really invigorating and a great workout. If you're feeling confident, add an arm movement or two such as harem (see page 65), or if you really feel up for it, the snake arms (see page 60)!

63

TRAVELING STEPS

Traveling steps makes movements more fun *and* more aerobic. They also enhance your grace, balance, and coordination; and will give you a more confident, sexy walk in everyday life.

— **Cross step:** Start by stepping your right foot across in front of the left, putting your weight on your right leg, and then extend the left foot out to the side. Repeat on the other side: Cross your left foot in front of the right, stepping onto the left foot, and extend your right leg while pointing the toe. Your knees bend slightly as you cross your legs and straighten as you extend your foot. You can also add snake arms (see page 60) with this movement. (On the DVD, you'll notice that we transfer our weight on the extended foot to give the full snake-arm extension.)

— **Forward-step-back-step (or four-count base):** This is exactly what it sounds like: Your right foot steps forward, left foot steps in place, right steps foot back, and left foot steps in place. That is, the right foot travels forward and back, while the left foot stays in the center. Try it slowly at first, and then go faster. Point the toes of the moving leg as your belly leads forward and back. Many arm movements can accompany this traveling step—we like adding snake arms.

— **Walking basic:** This is another commonly used traveling step in belly dance. First, step with your right foot and extend your left leg out in front while twisting your left hip upward, keeping the front toes pointed. Now step with your left leg and extend the right one, twisting and lifting your right hip. Step as you travel forward, keeping your arms out to the side. When you feel comfortable, extend your arms to genie (see page 65) as you travel.

— **Hagala:** There are three basic parts to this one: (1) Begin by stepping forward with the right leg, bending your front leg, and keeping your weight on the back (left) leg; (2) shift your weight from the back to the front leg with your hips; and (3) bring your back leg all the way around and step forward by lifting your hip, and then start the process all over. Shift your weight, lift from your belly and step . . . shift, lift, step . . . shift, lift, step. Lead with your belly and hips, not your legs, and keep your back leg straight. This is also known as the "three-quarter-shimmy walk."

— **Four-step turn:** Turns are very common these days in belly dance. If you've had any kind of dance training, they'll come to you quite easily. First, step out to the side with your right foot, putting weight on it. Pivot on your right foot as you step and transfer your weight to your left foot, turning halfway, so that your back is facing the audience. Then step out with your right foot again, putting your weight on it as you pivot and turn halfway, completing the turn and facing the front. Then extend the left foot.

Try it again: Step right, pivot half turn, step left, pivot half turn, step right, touch left. To do the same turn in the other direction, just start with the opposite foot: Step with your left foot, putting weight on it. Then pivot on your left foot as you step and transfer your weight to your right foot, turning halfway toward the back; then step out with your left foot, putting your weight on it as you pivot and turn halfway, completing the turn and facing the front. Left, pivot, right, pivot, left, touch. Try alternating: right turn, then left turn.

ADDING ARMS

While you're practicing and perfecting your dance workout, try accentuating those movements with beautiful arm positions. Your arms and shoulders express grace and fluidity in belly dance. The arm movements can also strengthen and stretch your upper body, which also helps you maintain good posture. The following are terms that Neena and I have created for easy reference.

— **Anwar arms:** Extend both arms up in the shape of the letter V, with palms facing inward toward each other and index fingers slightly pointed. This finger position indicates unity in Islamic prayers. Try these arms with a four-step turn. This can also be done with palms facing outward.

— **Serpent arms:** Place one arm above your head, palm curved downward; and bring your other arm down to your side, palm curved inward, framing your hips and making the shape of the letter S. Now switch arms. This is a great arm position for accentuating movements such as hip drops and hip dropkicks (see page 62). Your lower arm frames the hip that's moving.

65

— **Harem arms:** Bring both hands to rest lightly at the back of your head, as if you're resting on a large pillow, and feel your body elongate along the sides of your torso. Initially, dancers may have developed this graceful movement to cool themselves by lifting their long hair off of their necks. Harem arms are a perfect combination with the hagala dance step (see page 65).

— **Cairo arms:** Extend your right arm in front of your body, and the left arm to the side, slightly below shoulder level in an L-shaped position. Be sure to square your shoulders evenly. Extend your arms away from your body and reach out through your fingertips, then switch sides. For variety, you may also do this position with one arm above your head instead of out in front, again forming an L shape. Try either style while traveling with a forward-step-back-step (see page 64).

— **Genie arms:** We often refer to these as "moving genie" because the arms alternate and move at the same time. Place one hand at your temple, palm facing outward, and extend your other hand out in front of you with the palm facing downward. Now switch arms and repeat, alternating arms. You may also do this step with one arm extending out to the side rather than in front of you. These movements are best done with the walking-basic travel (see page 64).

— **Duniya arms:** *Duniya* means "world" in Arabic (and also in the Hindi language). With your left arm out to the side, sweep right arm horizontally in front of your head and around the back of your head, moving your arm all the way around and landing in Cairo arms. Now, do the same on the other side: The left arm sweeps all the way around. Make sure to keep both arms extended and your spine long, with shoulders relaxed down. Neena and I love this move with a four-step turn (see page 65).

Veils

Using a veil when you dance adds an elegant grace to your arm movements, mystique to your image, and an extra challenge to your workouts. Depending on the fabric, the veil may have a slight weight to it, or may be as light as the wind. Each one has its own uniqueness, which is expressed by the dancer. The veil is an extension of her—it's mystical, sensual, graceful, and fun, and it adds to the satisfaction and pleasure of the workout. Muscle control keeps the veil movements smooth and flowing, and it means that you're training your mind and body to move in a more graceful, yet powerful way.

Veils are usually two and a half to three yards of flowing, drapey fabric. Hold your veil with your arms extended so that it's even and taut. You can either grasp it between your index and middle fingers or between your middle and ring fingers. Cup the other side of the fabric with your thumb.

Now you're ready to learn some exciting movements. Think of your veil as an extension of your arms as you try some of our favorite steps. Do them slowly at first, and when you feel comfortable with them, increase your speed. Then you might want to try some of the other movements in this chapter with your veil as well, to give your workout more variety.

— **Anwar veil:** You already know this one: Just do anwar arms (see page 64) while holding your veil. This is one our favorite entrance steps. As you walk, notice how the fabric waves behind you; and when you add the four-step turn, this movement displays power and elegance.

— **Aladdin veil:** Standing in belly pose (see page 57), extend one arm out to the side, and put the other on the back of your head. Now create a figure eight with your extended arm, and be sure to point your unweighted toe. For this step, you can imagine that the veil is an extension of your long, flowing hair.

— **Caravan:** By adding a cross step (see page 63) to the Aladdin veil, you create the caravan. This is one of my favorite classic veil movements.

— **Red sea:** This is also known as "ocean." Extend both arms out at shoulder level, holding your veil. Then cross, step to the right and cross, step to the left. This is a fun, grand movement for any choreography!

ULTIMATE UNDULATIONS (THE CAMEL): THE BELLY-DANCE MOVE THAT WILL TRANSFORM YOUR ABS—AND YOUR SEX LIFE

Belly dance in general can boost your sexual self-confidence as well as your technique in bed. But the undulation (or "camel") is something even more: It's a complete movement—a full-body exercise that works many of your major and minor muscles from head to toe. It particularly works the entire pelvic region, the hips, and the upper- and lower-abdominal muscles. So forget about those tired old sit-ups and undulate yourself to firm abs!

One of our master teachers from Egypt called the undulation the absolute best exercise movement for women. Whether you're about to have a baby or interested in a more exciting, satisfying sex life, this classic belly-dance move is the ultimate in sensuality, and it gives you exquisite control over your body when it counts!

There are different ways of approaching this movement, because it can be a little challenging. But we've found this method to be pretty simple. We'll break the step down into its main parts and then show you how to put them together in one smooth, sinuous movement. (You may want to stand in front of a full-length mirror to see what you're doing.)

We'll begin with the first part: Turn to one side, facing the corner for a better view of your body. Then go to what Neena and I call the "Egyptian stance," which is one foot in front of the other, about two to four inches past the heel, keeping both feet parallel, "pharaonic" style. (It doesn't really matter which foot is in front. I like to start with my right foot if I'm facing the left corner.)

Next, step forward and back, rocking your weight to your front foot and then the back one, allowing a slight bend in both knees.

Start leading with your belly, and your hips will naturally follow. Your belly leads forward as you rock your weight toward the front foot, hips and knees follow; and then the belly leads back as you rock your weight backward . . . and hips and knees follow once more. Do this movement a few times until you feel comfortable. You've already created a basic lower undulation!

To include the upper body, lead with your heart as your rib cage slides forward. Notice how your belly, hips, and knees naturally follow like a train, again allowing your weight to rock forward onto the front foot. Now, lift your rib cage up toward the sky, stretching the sides of your upper body. Circle your chest around and back as you complete this circle, allowing the chest to lead, contracting first your upper abs, then the lower ones. Notice again how your belly, hips, and then knees follow as you rock your weight gently to the back leg.

Try it again: Leading with your chest, slide the ribs forward and up as you rock your weight forward. Your belly and then hips follow the ribs, completing your upper-rib circle. Then rock your weight backward to the back foot; again, belly and then hips follow. You've just done an undulation!

Bigger movements are created with large upper body circles, and smaller ones with small circles. By increasing your speed, notice how the undulation can become smaller and more concentrated. This movement can be done in place or as you walk (when it becomes a traveling step).

Belly Breathing

Whew! That was quite a workout, wasn't it? Let's cool down now with belly breathing, a technique that relaxes and oxygenates your entire body with tension-free, deep breathing.

Begin by lying on your back. For physical awareness of your belly, you can rub your hands together until they're somewhat warm, and place one hand on top of your midriff. Notice how your hand rises and falls as you inhale and exhale.

As you breathe deeply into your abdomen, find any tension in your body and release the tightness and stress with each breath, starting with your forehead . . . moving to your jaw, then the neck and shoulders. . . . Relax your arms, hands and fingers . . . then your legs, feet, and toes. Breathe deeply into the lower belly, and breathe out any unwanted tension.

Belly breathing alone will revive and energize you, and you can transfer that same feeling of relaxation as you sit up in a cross-legged position. Keeping your "sit bones" firmly planted on the ground, allow your spine to naturally grow and elongate upward, beginning at the belly and going all the way to the crown of the head. Let your hips and shoulders naturally release away from each other.

Continue with that same feeling as you stand, arms relaxed by your sides. Send your belly breath into any tension spots, and feel as if your spine is growing upward as you breathe naturally. Allow your hips and legs to feel as if they're dangling from your belly.

Next, take a little walk, and feel the freeness in your stride. You'll notice your awareness expanding, because there's no tension to block it. (Don't forget to incorporate your belly posture when you're walking!)

Belly-Dance Workout Tips and Pointers

Your workout will be safe, effective, and enjoyable if you follow these guidelines:

— **Set goals.** How much you exercise and what you want to achieve is up to you. The general rule is this: Depending on your body type, work out at least one hour, three to five days a week if you want to lose weight; and at least one half-hour, three to five days a week for health benefits, sculpting, and toning. You might need more or less, depending on your individual metabolism, what you eat, your other physical activity, and your goals. Just remember: Anything is better than nothing! If all you can do is ten minutes, then do ten minutes.

— **Schedule time.** You don't need to do your entire workout all at once if you can't carve out a big enough chunk of time. Do 10, 15, or 20 minutes at a time, as long as it adds up to your goal time at the end of the day. You might do the lower body and undulation workout in the morning for 10 to 15 minutes, take a 10- to 15-minute walk at lunchtime, and then do the traveling steps and undulation for 10 to 15 minutes in the evening.

— **Listen to your body.** If you're not used to moving much, start slowly and easily and pay attention to how your body feels. Beginners may feel a little tired at first, but this will pass, and you'll soon feel that good belly-dance energy as you work out and during the rest of the day. If you feel a little sore at first, know that this will be temporary—and can also mean that it's working! Your muscles are getting a workout and with repetition, you should see great results. Keep dancing, and take a muscle-soothing bath.

— **Stay with it.** Some belly-dance movements might feel slightly awkward or difficult at first. Stick with it as you listen to the music and let your body flow to the beat. You'll get into it eventually, and then the movements will feel natural and exhilarating.

— **Music.** It's possible to do your workout without music, but many of the steps are more fun and easier to do if you play some music to accompany you, because it keeps you motivated. Play any kind, as long as it inspires you to move. At first, Western songs, with their familiar rhythms, may make it easier for you to stay on the beat. Later, you can graduate to Arabic tunes; there are plenty to choose from on the DVD.

— **Workout wear.** You don't need special belly-dance gear to do these steps, although costumes do add to the fun and fantasy. For now, just choose something that's comfortable, lets you move, and makes you feel feminine and beautiful. My sister and I wear leggings and midriff-baring tops in our instructional videos, but you don't have to expose your belly if you don't want to. However, when you get to the undulation, revealing your stomach will allow you to see your progress more clearly. We do recommend that you tie a scarf around your hips to accentuate their movements and to get you in the mood. Any fabric will do, but most of our students eventually want to buy a hip scarf with, sparkling golden coins.

— **Expand your repertoire.** Once you get the hang of these basics, we encourage you to explore our additional belly-dance workouts and choreography on DVDs and videotapes, if you haven't already, or try attending belly-dance classes in your local area. You can always learn more, and classes give you something extra: individualized feedback from the instructor and the camaraderie and encouragement of other women.

71

— **Have fun and let go!** Don't think so much when you dance—instead, get in touch with your inner belly and let go of those inhibitions as if you were a kid again. Feel your midsection as the foundation from which all the movement emanates, not your head. After all, it's called *"belly* dance," not *"brain* dance"!

Shape Your Body, Shift Your Life

Now that you know some key belly-dance movements, you'll see that this art form is a fantastic body shaper—in fact, you'll be able to feel the difference after your very first workout! Through belly dancing regularly, you'll achieve the body and weight that's uniquely right for you. And in a little while, you'll notice that the dancing is sneaking into the rest of your life. You'll see other changes, such as a special type of energy, attitude, awareness, grace, and confidence in your movements—even in something as simple as walking.

If you do go to the gym to lift weights, you'll be more aware of your posture, alignment, pace, and form. Believe it or not, biceps curls and sit-ups can have rhythm and style! In fact, belly dance can help you look at all forms of physical activity through new eyes, and inspire you to live a more active life—whether it's biking, gardening, skating, hiking, yoga, or even other types of dancing.

Try some belly-dance moves to freshen and spice up your style when you're having a night on the town. The next time you're at a party or in a dance club, surprise everyone with a couple of hip drops and some shimmies on the dance floor. There's so much world beat being played these days that it's natural to allow the music to inspire you to add a little exotic style to your usual moves.

And don't laugh, but belly-dance attitude can even transform mundane tasks such as housework into a fun workout. When Neena and I were kids, even chores were play to us. When we had to clean up, we'd make a dance out of scrubbing the floors. We used rubber bands to attach sponges to the bottoms of our feet and scrubbed the floor by doing choo-choo shimmies (great for thighs and hips!). When we dusted, we'd do long, sweeping arm motions that we discovered later were great for our upper-body muscles. We even established a rhythm while washing dishes or vacuuming. Sometimes we even pretended to be ballerinas and put one foot up on the sink to get a great hip stretch. Today, my housekeeper does most of the cleaning, but when she's not here, I still choo-choo around to clean the floor, and use snake arms to dust the furniture and wipe the countertops.

Twirling and singing through life is nothing new. Traditional songs and dances in most cultures were inspired by daily activities such as harvesting, farming, fishing, fetching water, herding sheep, and courtship—and belly dance is no different. It's an expression of women's emotions and the ways of their lives. For example, there are Egyptian-style dance movements used today that are inspired by everyday living in Egypt: herding sheep, fishing, flirting, and even shopping in an open market!

The more you move, the more toned and shaped you'll be, and the more confidence movement will give you. That can change your life in every area—from relationships to your career to inner happiness. And the habit of being physically active helps you get going in other aspects of your life. Belly dance and other movements represent the changes you want to make in all the other parts of your life, including what you eat, what you wear, the way you do your hair and makeup, and how well you take care of yourself. Speaking of which . . . it's spa time!

* * *   * * *

Chapter Five

PAMPER YOUR BELLY . . .
LIFE AS A LUXURY SPA
BY NEENA

Eastern cultures say that your body is a temple and that you must take care of it. So whether you've worked out with belly dance or worked yourself into a frenzy on the job, you deserve to relax and give yourself a gift. Spa treatments are relaxing, beautifying, and rejuvenating; they're instant mood makeovers that transport you to a world of sensual delights that really gets your motor purring. Since the belly way is a lifestyle of feel-good luxury, it's not surprising that spa-type methods go a long way back in many belly-dance cultures, and that many retreats are offering these dance classes as part of their services.

You might think that massages are a total indulgence and that they're only for the rich. That's what Veena and I used to believe, too, until we discovered that women really *need* to be pampered and take care of themselves. Having a massage, a facial, or some other type of spa treatment regularly can (and will) take years off your life. Not only will your insides thank you, but your skin will have a youthful glow—and all without painful, expensive surgery! What's more, massages are sensual, so after your treat, think about how you'd love to give a similar gift to your significant other.

Back in the days when Veena and I performed six nights a week until all hours, if I didn't have a deep-tissue massage by Monday, it would have been pretty difficult for me to continue with the shows. Afterward, I felt so rejuvenated and ready to take on the world that those appointments became a necessity!

It began about eight years ago, when my sister and I were performing in Hong Kong and staying at a five-star hotel that offered spa services. That's where I had my first spa experience, even though so many of my friends had told me that I must try it because it's unbelievably relaxing and pampering. We'd been working hard, and I decided to indulge myself, so I made an appointment for a massage—and whoa! It *did* feel great, and the way the staff fussed over me made me feel even more special. I loved it so much that I booked one for Veena right away.

Soon after, I stayed for a long weekend at a spa in the beautiful rolling hills of the wine country in Napa Valley. That time I had a Swedish massage and a eucalyptus steam . . . and before I knew it, I was hooked!

Since then, my sister and I have had a whole variety of treatments, including facials and all types of tension-melting massages; we've had streams of hot oil poured on our foreheads (*verrry* relaxing); and we've been scrubbed with salt, slathered with mud, and wrapped mummy-style in herbs. We've been steamed, baked, and soaked in hot water strewn with rose petals.

For a long time, I associated these luxuries with going on a trip to get away from it all—but that ended when Veena and I discovered day spas. Now I can go on a mini-vacation without leaving the city or bothering with packing, expensive airfare, hotels, and restaurants! What's more, I don't have to use the excuse that "I just don't have the time" or "I can't get away from work for a week."

Among the variety of items on a menu of spa treatments, what I crave most of all are massages. Maybe because I'm a dancer, constantly giving my body a workout, or because I sit for hours in airplanes and am under the mental stress of running a business . . . whatever the reason, I need my rubdown fix! I feel fortunate that my sister's and my work often takes us to exotic places all over the world, which affords us the opportunity to try different styles of massage.

It's interesting that every culture has developed its own wonderful and effective techniques for body work. We've been "spa-ed" in the U.S., India, Egypt, and throughout Europe and the Middle East—practically all over the world. While we haven't had it all, we sure have tried a lot: the long, soothing strokes of Thai massage; the "good pain" pummeling of deep tissue and sports rubdowns; and the rejuvenating, therapeutic effects of many Asian styles such as Tibetan pulsing and Ayurveda.

I've come to realize that this kind of luxury is a necessity, especially for women. We carry so much emotional "junk" and "baggage" in our bodies, and relaxing procedures release all of that, leaving our essence: the inner child. This playful, joyful, uninhibited girl inside each of us makes us beautiful women. When this is present in you, creativity radiates from your body, bringing out the sensuality and femininity in every way. One time, after my favorite treatment, I decided to get up and dance to some new music that I'd never heard. My body just soared with flowing movements . . . it was heaven.

Soooo, whether you splurge on a sumptuous vacation or are a do-it-at-home type of gal; whether you want to rest, relax, and recharge your batteries or rev up your sexual energy; whether you want to jump-start life changes or drop a few pounds and firm a few inches . . . listen to that voice inside you that's saying, "C'mon, let's go!"

Amazing Options

There are more than 10,000 spas in the U.S. and Canada. If you went to one of these every day for the next 30 years, you might cover them all—so you'd better start soon! The most luxurious of all are the resort or destination types. Like heavenly little self-contained villages, they lavish you with attention and offer everything under the sun. Often situated in places with views to die for, lots of other activities, and a healthy environment to immerse yourself in, these are perfect escapes for hardworking women or couples who want a romantic getaway.

Choose from beach resorts with ocean vistas and the gentle sounds of lapping waves; desert or mountain retreats with clear, crisp air; or even floating spas on luxury cruise ships. These are the places to totally indulge yourself with massages and baths; beauty treatments such as facials, manicures, and pedicures; fresh, light, pure food that's designed to knock off a few pounds and introduce you to a new way of eating; exercise such as aerobics, swimming, dancing, hiking, and yoga; detoxification through exfoliation, brushing, saunas, wraps, and steam; and mind-body techniques that include deep breathing and meditation.

In addition to resorts, there are many luxury hotels that offer a menu of massages, facials, steams, saunas, manicures, and pedicures. If you're interested in both an inner and outer transformation, there are also wellness or fitness getaways that will help teach you a healthier all-around lifestyle. Day or beauty spas offer services without the overnight accommodations. And the latest addition is the mobile unit: professionals (working either solo or in teams) who essentially bring a day spa to your home and take the hassle out of getting there and back again. They even bring their own atmosphere: candles, aromatherapy supplies, plush robes, and music. You can also join the trend and try a spa party by inviting a group of friends over to while away the hours as you're pampered together.

A Trip Back to Ancient Times

North America has modern Western facilities, but a trip to a spa in a Middle Eastern country can be like a journey back in time. The original ancient therapies were mineral waters and hot springs. (Veena and I still enjoy these healing waters today.) The idea of using water and heat to relax, heal, and detoxify is traditional in many cultures. These two elements—in the forms of baths, steam rooms, and saunas—are still a mainstay in most spas in the Middle East.

Perhaps nothing exemplifies this ancient heritage like the traditional Turkish baths. Although early Arabs were accustomed to washing themselves with cold water, they never sat in a bath. Heat won over cold when conquering Arabs learned the pleasures of soaking in hot water from the ancient Greeks and Romans. The Turkish bath, called *hammam* ("spreader of warmth") in Arabic, was forbidden to women at first, but eventually the ladies were allowed their own time slots.

In time, trips to the baths became so important to Muslim women that if husbands denied them this right it was considered grounds for divorce! (Are you listening, guys?) Most Islamic cities in Iran, Asia Minor, Africa, Egypt, and Morocco have some hammams, but today they're rare in Turkey, except in the larger hotels. Despite this, women young and old still enjoy these traditional centers. The older ones visit to maintain their youth—and sometimes to try to find a potential wife for their son.

India, too, has a long tradition of spa-type treatments that goes back for thousands of years. Traditionally, *ashrams* (monastic retreats) were all the rage as the place to go for purification treatments called *panchakarma*. These included massage, steam, exfoliation, special foods and herbs, and other practices. This was a rather rigorous program, and traditionally, purification was recommended with the change of every season.

Today you can find traditional Ayurvedic health resorts that combine modified Indian traditions with more luxurious Western spa therapies. Some of the greatest massages that Veena and I experienced were in India; in fact, she had her first massage at a day spa in Delhi (well before I finally indulged in Hong Kong). The Ayurvedic approach is designed to balance the energy in the whole body, so it's a whole different vibe than other styles. The practitioners concentrate on working the *marma* points (energy points, similar to those in shiatsu).

In addition, India, Egypt, and the Middle East are very much into using oils to massage and lubricate the skin. In India, sesame oil in particular is believed to calm frazzled nerves, balance hormones, help with detoxification, and counteract stress. So on top of using massage oil to work your muscles, these spas offer a special procedure called *shirodhara* (shir-oh-DAH-rah), which involves pouring a steady stream of warmed oil on your third eye (located on your forehead) for about 30 minutes. Ayurveda believes this point to be the part of the brain where higher states of emotions and thoughts are processed.

My sister and I find that shirodhara deeply relaxes the muscles of our face and scalp so that any stress locked up there just melts away. This is so awesomely soothing that Veena always falls asleep—and she doesn't even care how much oil gets into her hair! It's a wonderful double whammy: a massage *and* hot-oil treatment!

Spas in Israel and other parts of the Middle East are big on thermo-mineral springs, which contain a high concentration of salt. They also emphasize treatments with black mud that's rich in minerals and absorbs toxins from your body—great for your circulation and strengthening your hair.

In Search of Spas

Spas are becoming more popular every year, so they're promoting themselves and are pretty easy to find. If you long for an exotic escape to experience Middle Eastern or Indian treatments firsthand, contact your travel agent or the tourist bureau of the country you want to visit. For a good Web listing, visit **www.spa-addicts.com,** which recommends facilities all over the world, many of which have been rated by users. A fun twist for your getaway—whatever its length—would be to find a place that offers dance lessons in addition to spa services!

Neena & Veena's In-Home Spa

By now we hope that you're sold on the idea of spas. But you might be thinking, *It's a little inconvenient at the moment to go running off to Istanbul or Palm Springs.* And perhaps a day spa or other alternative doesn't appeal or is still out of your price range. Relax . . . we're going to guide you through setting up your own at-home spa!

First, set the stage by conjuring up a feast for all your senses: Create an opulent, spalike atmosphere with sensual relaxing music (I recommend an Arabic *taksim:* a relaxing nonrhythmic music of violins, oud, or other solo instruments; see page 41 for more information), fluffy towels, a silk robe, fresh flowers, scented candles, and potpourri. If you desire, splurge on a vase of peacock feathers, wall-hanging rugs, a potted indoor palm tree or two, and even a small portable water fountain or bamboo screen. Go as far as you want and as far as your budget allows. You might even want to do a mini-makeover in one part of your home, painting the walls in restful earth tones and switching to more soothing lighting. For example, Veena's bedroom and one of her bathrooms look like part of one of the spas we visited in Egypt.

Affordable Luxury

It's true: Spas aren't cheap. If price is an issue, there are lots of ways to make the experience more affordable. For instance, although a vacation away from home is ideal, day spas are popping up everywhere in malls and downtown locations. You can spend as much or as little time there as you want: 30 minutes, an hour, a day, or anything in between. These businesses usually offer packages (such as a combination of a massage, facial, manicure, and so on) for a lower fee than if you bought these services individually.

Veena and I visit day spas about twice a month. We have either a massage or reflexology (stimulation of specific points on the feet that affect the whole body) and a salt scrub. Really, it still feels like a mini-vacation, even if it's only for a day or half a day. So treat yourself for your birthday . . . or just because!

Health clubs also offer massages. When you pay for one, you usually also get to take

79

movement classes and use the rest of the facilities that day, such as the pool, exercise equipment, sauna, steam room, and Jacuzzi. Another possible cost saver, depending on where you live, is to visit an Asian community with spa-type facilities that offer Japanese, Thai, or Chinese massage; reflexology; and sometimes steam treatments, a sauna, and hot and cold baths. These are usually less expensive than their Western-type equivalents. Yet another option is to go to a massage school, where you'll get worked on by students who need to put in a certain number of practice hours. (Don't worry—they're usually supervised.)

I've had bodywork at an Ayurvedic school, and although the practitioner didn't have that finesse that comes with years of practice, I still felt so relaxed that I fell asleep. And I stayed calm when I got the bill: half the usual price! Another time, both Veena and I went to a Western-style student masseur. He was so fresh out of the starting gate that he put his notes from class on Veena's back so that he could read them while he worked on her—and we had a pretty good laugh over that. Now the same guy is in such demand that we have trouble getting an appointment!

Another quick, ten-minute refresher is available from the masseuses that work at local health-food or outdoor markets. I've tried it a couple of times, and although I'd much rather not have all the foot traffic going by while I'm sitting in the chair being pummeled, it really does the job for the tiny little stresses, aches, and fatigue that come from everyday living—and it's very inexpensive!

The downside of these alternatives to regular spas is that there's little or no ambience, and you might need to wait a bit for your turn. But they're clean (which is what really matters), and you'll get some of the same benefits as with the full treatment, so if that's the only way for you to get your pampering—go for it! I've never regretted choosing these options in the past, and I still enjoy them now. With a little planning, you can have plenty of luxury when you get home by taking a decadent bath surrounded by candles and incense.

Rx: Hands-On Tension Relief

Massage not only feels good—it *is* good for you. All the world over, massage is known to be an effective tension reliever. And when you're relaxed, you look better and stay younger longer—nothing accelerates premature aging faster than stress! When stress hormones increase and stay elevated, muscles begin breaking down and so does collagen, which is the "glue" that holds tissues together and keeps them looking smooth and young.

And if you're physically active, as we are, you need a regular massage to keep your body in working condition.

So don't feel a bit guilty about pampering yourself, because managing stress beautifies you inside and out. Like a dancer, you need to feel good in order to perform your best: You'll sleep better and have more energy, and people will appreciate you more because they'll see you at your best.

Next, decide which of the at-home treatments (page 79) you want to try, and get your supplies ready. We generally like to use natural products such as avocados, fruits, honey, milk, oatmeal, sea salt, chickpea flour, turmeric, herbs, flower petals, and apple-cider vinegar. But if you have a favorite store-bought version of a product that you prefer, go ahead and use it. More and more manufacturers are incorporating natural ingredients these days, and most spas emphasize these products and scents.

My sister and I started using natural alternatives a long time ago, when we were still living with our parents. One of our mother's Indian friends was into saving everything, especially seen-better-days food such as overripe fruits and avocados. I can still hear her saying, "Don't throw out that avocado—put it on your hair! Don't toss that bruised banana—put it on your face!" If we'd accidentally cracked eggs, she'd remind us: "Don't get rid of them—shampoo them right into your hair!"

There were always vegetable oils around the house, and my sister and I used them to make a little something to shine up our hair. What started as an economic way to use things that were no longer good for eating became a way of life as we found that these gifts of nature really worked and made delightfully sensual and fragrant spa products. The skin can absorb chemicals; and we like to put pure, natural food in our bodies—so why wouldn't we want the same quality for our outsides?

Now, look at your calendar and try to set aside *one entire day* for yourself so that you can create a time oasis to go with the physical one you're going to experience. If this isn't possible, block out at least three hours. It may seem decadent to reserve one day a week—but that's the idea! So try to make time every week for one spa treatment, even if it's just a bath or a facial. In ancient times, the Arabs used to say, "Whoever goes to the bath on 40 consecutive Wednesdays will succeed at anything they do." Now, it doesn't have to be a bath, and it doesn't have to be Wednesday . . . but you get the idea.

Head-to-Toe Ancient Spa Treatments

Here are the basics about some of our favorite ways to pamper our body, face, hands, and feet. We've also included a special Neena & Veena's Salon section in the Appendix (page 167) with the specific recipes for our best beautifying concoctions. You can refer to those pages over and over as your own personal recipe book after you've gotten some great ideas from this chapter.

DREAMY BATHS

More than any other spa treatment, a bath can transport you to another world. Bathing has a long tradition in the Middle East and India—in fact, immersion in the Ganges River is an important ritual with Hindus. From relaxing to rejuvenating to just plain pleasurable, submerging yourself in warm water mixed with natural ingredients is a time-tested way of pampering.

Bear in mind that if your skin tends to be on the dry side, take your bath with warm rather than very hot water, and limit your soaking to 10 or 15 minutes. Pat yourself dry gently and immediately apply a soothing body lotion because that's when the skin absorbs it best. If you feel like it, you can also put some leave-in conditioner in your hair before you begin, cover with a plastic shower cap, and let it work its magic as you soak.

AROMATHERAPY

Smell is a powerful sense that evokes strong memories. We once met a woman in Egypt who ground up herbs and flowers, and we almost swooned when she made one of our favorite scents from rose petals. Now, whenever we put rose water on our veils and take a whiff, it transports us right back to Egypt. Every time we smell jasmine, it takes us to India, where women perfume themselves with strings of real jasmine flowers. We love real flowers because they're so natural and so sensual, and they're good for the soul.

Spas usually include some form of aromatherapy in their services, and one easy way to duplicate this in your home is with fresh or dried herbs, fresh flowers, or essential oils. For an herb-scented bath, make a strong cup of tea (using tea bags, not loose tea) and add that to the bathwater. You can also place a handful of fresh or dried herbs in a square of cheesecloth or plain muslin. Tie the ends together and let the bag steep in the bathwater, just like a tea bag.

To use essential oils, add about ten drops of your favorite type to the bath. Of course, for the ultimate in luxury, you can buy fragrant flowers or rose petals, which our ancient friend Cleopatra used in her bath along with milk. It must have been quite pretty, as well as aromatic.

SILKENING SCRUBS

Some women are born with silky skin and a radiant, healthy glow, while others need a little help to get that way. But whatever skin type we have—normal, dry, oily, or sun-damaged—most of us can benefit from exfoliation. That's why many professional spas offer some type of treatment to stimulate circulation, banish the buildup of dead skin cells, remove accumulated grime, and help keep pores unclogged.

For the face, exfoliation doesn't need to involve using an abrasive tool (such as a loofah or a brush) that works well on the body. Sometimes I use a washcloth on my face, but I make sure to use a fresh one every time. (We'll discuss more ways to care for your face later in this chapter.)

There are many ways to exfoliate the body, but my favorite at-home method is with scrubs while I either bathe or shower. Commercial versions are available in pharmacies, bath-and-body shops, and health-food stores, but it's also easy and economical to make your own fresh potions. Check out our favorite exfoliating recipes in the Salon section of the Appendix (page 167). I particularly like salt, sugar, oatmeal, or ground apricot pits for exfoliating the body.

Veena got me hooked on salt scrubs, and now I use them whenever I take a shower in order to immediately feel as though I'm back in a spa. They have natural ingredients and really cool fragrances (such as pumpkin pie, green tea, and lime) that change my mood every time I'm showering, so they're also a form of aromatherapy.

And these products do more than clean your outer layer of skin: They work on an energetic level to purify your aura and take away any negative energy. When you've been through an upsetting experience or exposed to unpleasant or pessimistic people, a salt scrub is a luxurious necessity. (There are sugar scrubs as well, but these are only beneficial externally.) There's something special about putting sea salt on your skin—maybe it's because of the special relationship that humans have with the salty sea. You really will feel like a new person.

Another reason that it's important to exfoliate often is that without this step, moisturizers and lotions won't penetrate your skin as well. If you've never tried a scrub, the idea of using what sounds like liquid sandpaper on your skin might be a bit scary, but don't worry: It's gentler than you think, and you'll love the results. (But don't use salt scrubs in areas where your skin is sensitive, or if you have any cuts or abrasions.) When you do this on a regular basis, think of the process as removing an outer layer that no longer represents the new you, like a snake shedding its too-small skin.

Using one of these products is easy: With your fingertips, simply rub the abrasive paste all over your body in a circular motion, using lighter pressure on the delicate areas and stronger pressure on the rougher spots such as your knees, the bottoms of your feet, and your elbows. Then rinse, and you'll be smooth and squeaky clean!

FOUR-STEP FACIALS

While you're luxuriating in your bath, why not give your face a treat? At-home facials consist of cleansing, exfoliating scrubs, and masks. If you like, add a mini-facial sauna for deeper softening and clearing your pores.

— **Cleansing:** If you don't wear a lot of makeup, cleansing can be a snap. Most days I just splash plain lukewarm water on my face and pat dry. But when I wear stage makeup, it's a different process. On those days, I first use apricot or almond oil on a cotton pad to gently wipe off lipstick and any glitter and waterproof makeup and mascara, followed with gentle cleanser that's soap-, fragrance-, and alcohol-free. Be sure to use a clean washcloth instead of your hands to remove every trace of dirt and makeup.

— **Facial scrub:** Depending on their texture (coarse granules are harsher), you can also use oatmeal- or chickpea-flour-based scrubs to exfoliate the skin on your face. Instant oatmeal has a finer texture than the old-fashioned kind, and there are also commercial scrubs specially formulated for the face. Make sure that you massage gently because this skin is more delicate than the rest of your body. Give your face a rinse when you finish, and you're ready for your facial sauna.

— **Mini-sauna:** Steam is an ancient and effective way to deep-clean your face. Plain-water vapor alone will help open pores, loosen blackheads, draw out pimples, and remove toxins. In India, specific fragrant herbs are added to the water as well.

To make the sauna, heat a quart of water in a saucepan. When it comes to a boil, put the pot on a table over which you can lean comfortably. (Be sure to use a trivet to protect the surface of the table from the heat.) Add a handful of dried herbs or ten drops of essential oils, lean over the pot so that your face enters the stream of vaporized water, and make a tent over your head with a bath towel to keep the steam from escaping. Steam your face for five to ten minutes.

Watch that you don't get your face *too* close, because the excess heat could cause scalding and broken blood vessels. Also, you shouldn't use a face sauna if you have sensitive skin, are pregnant, or suffer from asthma.

Here are some ingredients that you can add to the water, as we mentioned above:

- **Normal skin:** lavender, sandalwood, fennel, rose, and licorice
- **Oily skin:** lemon, rosemary, bergamot, and dashmoola
- **Dry skin:** chamomile, orange peel, and neroli

In addition to its other benefits, the sauna prepares your face for a mask, allowing its nutrients to penetrate better.

Marvelous Masks

The next step is to apply a mask. Those made of simple, natural ingredients do a great job of moisturizing, taming acne and excess oil, slowing the development of wrinkles and nourishing the skin. The Salon lists recipes using fruits that have particular effects (page 170), but you can include any fruit for its skin-smoothing and mild-exfoliating effects. You may use just the juice or include the pulp, too. If you add pulp, be sure to cover your face with a piece of cheesecloth (cut out holes for your eyes and mouth) and apply the mask over it. Rinse off the mask with tepid or cool water, and gently pat your skin dry; then apply your favorite moisturizer.

85

Caring for Your Delicate Eye Area

For many people, the eye area is a major problem. You may have dark circles, making you look haggard; or you may retain fluid, making you look puffy; or you may be seeing early signs of aging. This is one of the first areas to show age, and it's also a problem area for fluid retention. Avoid salty foods and lack of sleep, which contribute to these problems, and follow these tips:

- Thin cucumber slices or grated cucumber and raw carrots are old remedies, but they're great standbys for reducing puffiness and soothing tired, sore eyes.

- Soak used tea bags in cold water for around ten minutes (making sure they're really cool) and place them on the puffy area.

❀ Cut a green grape in half and press it onto your skin, leaving as much juice and pulp behind as you can. Pay special attention to the area where crow's-feet form. Leave on for 20 minutes and then rinse.

❀ Place a slice of raw potato (or grated raw potato) underneath your eyes to lighten dark circles.

TENDER HAND AND FOOT CARE

Everyone focuses on the body and face as the main performers in life and love, but don't forget your hands and feet! In belly dance and in the bedroom, your feet are exposed and your hands are used for expressive movement. So for head-to-toe appeal, cared-for, pampered hands and feet are a must. Plus, these are probably the hardest-working parts of your body—and the most abused by tight shoes, work, and weather.

The last time we looked, our hands and feet were connected to our bodies, so it's no wonder that when they're unhappy, so are we. Try babying your feet with a massage—generously pour massage oil all over those tired, aching tootsies. After all, they work hard for you! For dancers, they're two of the most important parts of the body, which is why Veena and I set aside time every week for a reflexology appointment. We also love the inexpensive luxury of getting manicures and pedicures, which always include a massage and moisturizing treatment. But at-home foot and hand soaks, massage, moisturizing, and exfoliating also keep these parts soft and pretty. Check out some of our great recipes in the Salon (page 169)!

Spa treatments are only one way to care for these parts of your body: Remember to keep your hands soft and smooth by wearing protective gloves when doing chores. And stamp out foot abuse by wearing comfortable shoes or going barefoot whenever possible.

Float Away with Belly Breathing and Meditation

Now that you're all clean, steamed, scrubbed, massaged, and moisturized, it's time to sink even deeper into relaxation. Belly breathing is one of our favorite relaxation techniques. You learned this technique in Chapter 4 (page 68) to prepare yourself for your belly workout, and it can also be used with a cooldown. Many spas include deep breathing and meditation sessions because they're so relaxing, so go ahead and do belly breathing as part of your at-home pampering—you'll be glad you did!

This process brings your awareness to your belly; and reduces anxiety, depression, nervousness, muscle tension, and fatigue. Shallow breathing, on the other hand, robs you of energy and causes mental and physical fatigue. It leaves behind stale air and waste products in your lungs and prevents you from getting fresh, revitalizing oxygen in your tissues. In addition, breathing into the base of your spine engages your first chakra—the center of health, security, and the earth—so you feel more grounded on the physical plane.

As you inhale and exhale slowly and deeply, imagine a wave of air entering and leaving your body. With each inhalation, take in restful energy; with each exhalation, let go of cares, worries, and fatigue. Imagine the breath entering every organ, bone, and cell, cleansing and revitalizing every inch of you. Do this for at least three minutes on the first day, and gradually increase it to ten minutes, or even more. You may play soft music in the background, listen to the water trickling softly in a fountain, or just enjoy the silence. Your mind and body will become more and more relaxed with each breath, as if all your worries were floating away on a fresh breeze

Meditation often goes hand in hand with deep breathing. Veena and I started our own form of this practice when we were little girls, without even knowing that's what we were doing! Our mother, who was from India, taught us how, because it's a way of life in her country. The practice didn't cost any money, yet it was so valuable. We were very young when she introduced us to the concept; we used her instructions as a starting point and taught ourselves to go to a deeper level. We thought meditation was so cool! We saw all these images and scenes in our imagination that we called "the movies in our minds."

So if you're interested in going beyond breathing as a relaxation technique, think about learning how to meditate. A simple form is to close your eyes and silently repeat a word or a phrase to yourself, such as "one" or "ohm"; there are also many books and CDs available that teach a variety of techniques.

Immerse Yourself in Nature

You don't have to plan a vacation to a destination spa to experience beautiful natural surroundings as part of your treatment. Depending on where you live, try to spend some of your spa day in nature. You can do this right in your own backyard, with plants, trees, flowers, singing birds, and other living creatures eagerly awaiting your viewing pleasure. Spend a lazy hour swinging in a hammock watching the clouds drift by. Or maybe you prefer a picnic in the park; visiting a nature preserve or botanical gardens; or a short drive to the mountains, lake, ocean, or another community resort.

We all need our nature breaks—our bellies tell us that we need to decompress and just chill. A gentle walk along the shore or among the softly swaying trees can be very calming and rejuvenating; the blues of the water and sky and the green of the leaves are relaxing to the eyes and the mind. A visit to the great outdoors can be, literally, a breath of fresh air for your body and soul.

In some cultures, bathing in the sun or moonlight is also considered to be therapeutic. In ancient Egypt, for example, the sun was a god and was worshiped as the source of all life. People sunbathed in order to honor and capture this natural form of energy. And in India, bathing in moonlight is part of the health tradition.

Most dermatologists recommend wearing sunscreen 365 days a year, so if you plan to spend time outside, wear it! You may want to test several brands first to see which one you like. Get at least SPF 15, which some liquid makeup and even many moisturizers have.

Personally, I don't like many sunscreens because they can be toxic, and I hate feeling greasy. The exceptions that I do use are the natural products that I buy at health-food stores. Another option is to internally take flax-seed oil and essential-fatty-acid supplements. Some people use pure shea butter from Africa as a great natural sunscreen, and studies show that taking beta-carotene also protects against sun damage while heightening a golden tan.

Although too much sun can be harmful, a little can be good for you, so sit or lie in the warm sunlight for just a few minutes a day. Veena and I love the sun, as do most people—it not only brightens the day, but also lifts our moods. In Egypt where belly dance is said to have originated, everyone gets *plenty* of sun! Traditionally, some of the women living in the Middle East had the right idea of protecting their faces and body from the sun with clothing because it was so relentlessly hot. And in the deserts of Rajasthan, India, the women shade their faces with a colorful *chuni* or *dupatta,* which are veils that go over the head, sometimes reaching down to the nose. But most of us don't live in the strong sun of the desert, so Veena and I find that the best protection is to wear a wide-brimmed hat, a thin-cotton long-sleeved top, and pants.

Exactly how much sun is beneficial—yet safe? This will vary from person to person depending on her diet and genes. Just remember to limit your exposure to the morning and/or late afternoon, and don't let yourself get sunburned!

Miraculous Sleep

Sleep is the best beauty treatment and energizer there is, but most American women are shortchanging themselves. Many people consider some extra shut-eye to be the biggest luxury of all—but it's really the biggest necessity! When we don't get enough, we feel draggy, it interferes with our work and energy, we can't concentrate as well, and we even get a little irritable and short-tempered . . . not very sexy! Too little sleep can also interfere with our digestion and hormones; and generally make our mind, body, and spirit feel and behave as if they were older.

You can tell if you're undernourished in this department if you need an alarm clock to get up every day, or even most days. (Of course, falling facedown in your pasta or forgetting to pick up the baby from day care are also hints!) So your final spa treatment is to go to bed early this evening and give yourself the gift of enough sleep every night. Turn off that TV and all of those lights . . . and have sweet dreams!

TIPS TO IMPROVE YOUR SLEEP

- Wind down and quiet your mind with belly breathing, low-key yoga, meditation, prayer, and/or an affirmation.

- Eat a light supper to avoid burdening your digestive system overnight.

- Avoid any sugar or caffeine in the evening.

- Keep the room as dark as possible to avoid disrupting the sleep chemicals melatonin and serotonin.

- Clear your bedroom of clutter and stimulating activities (except for sex!).

- Exercise regularly, but not late at night.

- Go to bed at roughly the same time every day.

Make Every Day a Spa Day

It's the belly way to live a full life, with ups and downs, times of stress, and moments of calm. I'd be lying if I didn't tell you that it's a major balancing act for Veena and me to manage our careers. Sometimes it seems that we don't have one spare minute, but we've learned how absolutely necessary it is to take some time out for ourselves.

Belly dance itself makes you feel good and can relax you, getting you to feel more comfortable with your body, and spa treatments extend and strengthen that feeling. They're more than a reward—they're a continuation of being in your body and enjoying sensual pleasures. Those sensual belly-dance movements to exotic music aren't too far removed from having a massage or taking a long, fragrant, luxurious bath. As a woman, you *need* to take care of yourself; it's not being selfish to want a bit of pampering or to let someone else take care of you. And some of the best news is that spa treatments are an exception to the rule that you need to suffer to be beautiful. On the contrary, massages, facials, baths, and the like make you feel *and* look good. Talk about a win-win situation!

Once you get a taste of what spa living can do for you, you'll be hooked just like my sister and I are. Set aside an hour to get a massage on one weekend, a facial on the next. Or why not make *every* day a spa day—or create at least one pampering moment? Take some downtime to recharge your batteries, such as a small break from work, belly breathing for ten minutes, or just a walk in a park.

Sometimes when Veena and I don't have time for a full-body massage, or even time at the day spa for a reflexology treatment. We just have a simple treatment to our shower or bath, such as a salt or seaweed scrub; aromatherapy, such as lavender, vanilla, or spicy-ginger scented candles; or soft music. Its still rejuvenating.

Even a simple splash of rosewater on your face is a lovely way to start the morning. So go ahead and indulge your sensual side daily. More often than in the past, try to say yes to more of what you like and crave. Your body, mind, friends, and employer—and your lover—will be glad you did.

Mmmm . . . now that your body is yummily smooth, relaxed, buffed, and polished, let's decorate it with the panache and style of a belly dancer!

Chapter Six

ADORN YOUR BELLY . . .
PLAYING DRESS-UP
BY VEENA

Sometimes I think that Neena and I might have been born wearing bangles and chiffon! Even as children, we were always raiding the magical recesses of our mother's closet, and emerging—tah-dah!—in beautiful saris and dresses. Neena loved it even more than I did: She'd layer one dress over another to combine the colors and get that over-the-top effect. One time when we were about seven years old, she came out wearing eight dresses all at once! Most of them were skirts (or *lehngas*) from India. She wanted a big, fluffy silhouette and twirled around and around, the fabrics puffing out like petals. "Look at me, I'm a lotus flower!" she yelled. I remember watching her dance in her exuberant creation . . . how the dress moved . . . how she moved the dress. . . . What an amazing sight!

Even back then, I think we had the "belly way" attitude about clothes, which has three main components that you can follow, too: (1) It's about bringing out the exotic look in every woman, which adds a unique quality to the way you dress—which, in turn, brings out the uniqueness in you. (2) It means always thinking of yourself as being onstage, which will help you realize that everything you wear makes a statement. (3) Most important, your outfits and your movements go together. Clothes definitely inspire you to move in a certain way, whether you're dancing, walking, or performing: You move in the clothes, and the clothes move you.

Today, I love playing dress-up in fancy stage costumes; and even when my sister and I have on everyday wear like jeans and a T-shirt, we wear them with a belly dancer's style and attitude. The go-for-it, look-at-me dance sensibility keeps us feeling feminine, unique, and attractive. What could be more ordinary than a pair of jeans? Yet accessorized with the right pair of earrings or a spangle-studded hip scarf borrowed from the belly-dance wardrobe, you can still stand out from the rest of the denim-wearing crowd. This principle holds true no matter what your real-world boundaries may be: From sweats to a business suit, you can look up-to-date and use your clothes as a way to express your identity.

What you wear on the stage of life—whether you're on the job, working out, or out for a night on the town—says something about you. Image and appearance count, and in a sense, everyone wears costumes every day. Even a monk who gives up so many earthly pleasures is making a statement with his simple robe. What you wear is a form of communication: Are you feeling careless, colorful, drab, outrageous, beautiful, sexy, no-nonsense, powerful, daring, or creative today? When a belly dancer comes out onstage, the first thing that people notice is what she's wearing, before she even starts to dance. As performers, we dress to impress, to be attractive, and to make a statement. You can—and should—too!

Bring Out the Uniqueness in Your Wardrobe

Most little girls play dress-up in Mommy's clothes, just as we did. Do you remember doing that? Now that you're all grown up—and maybe even a mother yourself—who says that playful delight has to stop? Life's too short for dull duds, so we're going to help you transform your wardrobe so that it's full of clothes that make you smile and feel like dancing. Free yourself from the safe world of beige and navy and the ominous confines of an all-black wardrobe—boring!

Clothing has the power to transform you and always makes a statement. Wearing the right outfit will make you look and feel great. Some combinations make me feel energetic, flirtatious, and strong, while in others I feel sexy and confident. Each is a reflection of my own inner vitality and personality.

You'll notice all clothing affects your posture and movement in different ways. Maybe some of your clothes inspire you to do slow undulations; others may even make you feel like shimmying. So get out there and show your stuff! Go on: Grab the gold lamé T-shirt and spring for that sequined scarf—live a little! Explore yourself, experiment, be inventive, and enjoy your beauty and sensuality. Don't be afraid to do a little snake arm with your clothing style and extend yourself, even just a little. Clothes are fun, and dressing up is a blast!

As belly dancers, every adornment on our costumes has its place, purpose, and meaning. Those tasteful little pearl earrings might be just the ticket for a business meeting, but on a date? Fuhgeddaboudit! Heck, now that I think it over, you might even try something a little flashier at work, too.

One photographer friend of mine told me, "Dressing conservatively never got me anywhere." When I first met her, I knew that she was bold, creative, and sensitive because her clothes said it all. She's walking art, and she always stands out in the crowd.

Even fitting in doesn't mean that you need to look like everyone else; you can be proper without sacrificing your own uniqueness. For example, I went to a barbecue with some friends last year, where everyone wore boring basic shorts and a T-shirt or tank top. *I* wore a slightly beaded tank (yummy!) and a funky pair of wraparound shorts that I'd made, dressing it all up with some jewelry and little gold sandals. It made a statement, yet it was still appropriate.

So, choose the costume for the occasion, but dress to please yourself first—with style, comfort, and color—and everyone else second. Chances are, if you dress only for others, you may not like your wardrobe. But if you feel good about what you're wearing, other people will probably admire it, too.

Of course, there *are* limits, and you'd probably be going overboard in the individuality department if you wore a beaded bra top to your next board meeting! The point is that uniqueness and adorning yourself *don't* have to be inappropriate.

A Peek into Neena & Veena's Boutique

I like to think of my closet as a boutique, one of those little shops with special clothes that are fashionable, and expresses my individuality. If you walk into such a store, you'll notice that most of them have their own unique style that they specialize in, whether it's young and hip or chichi and frilly. They make you wonder what the owner is like. If my closet or Neena's was one of those boutiques, you'd definitely find a part of us—our belly essence—in everything from workout wear to everyday casuals. We get our inspiration from our hundreds of costumes, pieces of jewelry, headbands, tiaras, scarves, veils, and saris that we've gathered from exotic locales such as Egypt, Syria, Morocco, Turkey, India, Saudi Arabia, Afghanistan, Lebanon, and Pakistan.

So many women struggle to put together outfits, and the effort robs them of energy rather than building them up, becoming a source of stress rather than creativity. Or else they just give up and wear the same old boring outfits day after day. I think this is because they haven't found their own belly essence in their clothes. But by following a few simple principles that Neena and I have learned over the years, dressing for comfort and success can be fun and easy, a source of joy rather than another crisis.

Starting tomorrow, you can begin to create your own boutique of clothes that allows your individuality to shine through. This will probably mean that you'll be tossing out certain items and then shopping for some that work better for you. Have no fear—we'll take you through this process in just five steps. But first, whether you're selecting clothing to get rid of, buy, or wear today, we need to explain six basic principles to consider: color, texture, fit, ease of care, flattery, and freshness.

1. COLOR: CREATE YOUR OWN PALETTE

When buying an outfit, Neena and I first pay attention to color. With our olive skin tone and dark hair, we look good in jewel tones such as turquoise, red, emerald green, purple, and blue, so we tend to stock our boutique with items mostly in these colors. Then we pick and choose among these surefire winners depending on the occasion and our mood. We usually pick shades that really stand out for performance purposes, and sometimes we'll think about what wearing a certain hue represents. For example, I'll wear hot and sexy ruby red when it fits my mood. If I feel down-to-earth, I'll wear jeans, usually dressed up a bit with a colorful or ethnic top and a pair of flashy earrings.

When belly dancers perform, the colors of our costumes have an effect on our audience. Through the way something looks on us onstage and how it makes the audience feel, we're communicating a creative statement about our mood. Imagine what you're saying through the ones you choose to wear: What about sizzling hot pink, virginal white, or naughty-girl black lace?

The colors that suit you best are those that work well with your skin color, eyes, and hair—and your personality. Skin tone is important, but don't let it limit you. For example, if you have yellowish skin so that yellow looks terrible on you, but you love it, there are ways of getting around this challenge. Basically, you can either wear a shade of yellow that has blue undertones; or you can separate the color from your face, such as wearing a flattering scarf with a pleasant yellow skirt. When you know what shades look best on you, then you can create your personalized palette of clothes. Then, no matter how hurried you are, you'll always find treasures in your closet.

Personally, I think wearing the right color is most important in clothes, and there's a science to choosing what looks flattering on you. If you know what your "seasonal" color category is—summer, autumn, winter or spring—that narrows down a lot in which colors you should choose. A color consultant can develop your personalized color profile which is based on your personal colors—that is, your skin pigmentation, hair, and eye colors. Red, for example, is inspired by the red in your skin tone. So if you blush, that's the basis for your related red. Generally speaking, the clothing colors you choose to wear should be just a little lighter or darker than your personal colors.

2. TEXTURE: STAY IN TOUCH

The way that a fabric caresses the skin needs to be soft and sensual. The texture gives me instant feedback as I move. When we wear costumes that feel soft and flow gracefully, it's so much easier for us to move in a smooth and sensual way.

96

When I'm not performing, I favor soft cotton knits because they're so comfy-cozy and nice to the touch, yet can still be suggestively clingy and sexy in a subtle and understated way. Silks and chiffons are also especially soft and have a feminine quality; they drape and move well. I particularly love silk because this fabric always feels creamy and luxurious on my skin, and makes me feel sensual from the inside out. Velvet, velour, chenille, and angora all have high touchability scores as well. Lamé fabric feels soft, too, and because of its metallic sheen, it's an attention getter!

On the other hand, stiff or scratchy fabrics are turnoffs. Even in winter, I usually avoid wool unless it's cashmere, or I'm wearing it on top of a comfortable cotton shirt.

3. Fit: Comfort or Effect?

For the right effect when you're moving, find fabric that cradles your curves. Like belly-dance costumes, your outfits need to be able to emphasize and bring out the shapes. Without that quality, how can your movements stand out? Whether you're being viewed from the front as you walk toward someone or from behind as you walk away, it's all about the sensual up-and-down movement of your hips.

Our belly-dance costumes are the same: They have to fit just right in order to emphasize our shimmies, hip drops, and snake arms. Sometimes a sequined and bejeweled bra can be stiff and heavy—but the fit and weight make us accentuate our dance steps differently from the way we move when we're in our workout clothes.

Each costume has a life of its own because of the fabric and weight. If a bra is too loose, the audience may not be able to see my isolated movements—or even worse, I might pop out. (I learned this lesson in one of my very first shows when my skirt was too loose and actually fell down during a shimmy!) And it's no fun if a belt is too tight or binding either.

Fortunately, there are comfortable costumes—most of them designed by Neena and me. And although it's become common for some performers in Egypt and Lebanon to wear sexy high heels, we prefer to dance the traditional way: in bare feet. How much more comfortable can you get? In addition, many dancers who need footwear but want the feeling of barefoot, wear a balletlike slipper, which is popular in Egypt, or hermes sandals, which have a "Greek" look. Sometimes we wear either of these and find them to be very cute, comfortable, and practical.

Similarly, living the belly way means being aware of how the fit of *your* clothing makes you feel, look, and move. Often, the right fit is really a balancing act between comfort and effect. One of Neena's friends told her that if something's uncomfortable, then it's the right thing to wear for going out because "fashion hurts." I guess we all have different tolerance levels for discomfort—I'm always amazed by women who can run around

in high heels all day long and never complain! And although Neena doesn't *seem* to mind wearing clothes and shoes that have discomfort written all over them, as long they create a certain effect, I'm more likely to opt for feeling good.

Still, my sister and I both agree that clothes can't be so uncomfortable as to make us miserable and unable to dance or move our best—it's just not sexy. Just as we eat food that makes us feel good, we also wear clothes that feel good to our bodies. Now, you might be willing to pour yourself into a snug dress and wear six-inch heels on a first date; but honestly, that's going to probably affect your mood, movement, and attitude.

4. Self-Flattery: Play Up Your Strengths

In this case, flattery *will* get you somewhere—you just have to decide what it is you want to accentuate: your statuesque height, your cute petiteness, your generous cleavage, your saucy hips and derriere, or perhaps your sensual belly? Flaunt it when appropriate! The belly-dance attitude is: "I may not be perfect, but *parts* of me are excellent!" Contribute to the beauty of the world—don't deprive it of your gifts.

For example, if you've got great legs, don't wear pants or long skirts all the time. And if you do wear a long skirt, make sure that it has a slit up the side, front, or back. If you're slim all over, you can wear diaphanous or highly textured clothes, and even lush layers that embrace your femininity without making you look like a powder puff. A slim woman can also wear clean, simple lines, allowing her face and hair to stand out more.

Low necklines and beautifully draped garments can emphasize a bustline—even a modest one—beautifully. Impressive décolletage sheathed in snug, glittery, or shimmery fabrics can't be ignored. For curvy types, outfits that are all one color and those with vertical lines (stripes, other patterns, or stitching) are slimming while curve enhancing. And if you're curvy but toned, don't shy away from shiny fabrics: They can emphasize your shapeliness even more. Wearing a silhouette with a fitted waist lends shape and definition to any woman, regardless of her size. If you have beautiful feet, wear strappy sandals as the weather allows.

On the other hand, you can deemphasize aspects of yourself that you'd rather not call attention to. For example, petites look elongated in heels, especially when the shoes are paired with skirts that hit just at the knee or long, wide-legged pants. In fact, high heels create the illusion of longer, thinner legs on anyone.

If you want to look slimmer, there are lots of ways to trick the eye: Choose a blouse or top that's cut slightly wider at the shoulders or with a sleeve seam that has slight gathers or a soft shoulder pad; wear dark colors or vertical lines (such as thin stripes) below the waistline, and light colors above; or sport A-line skirts of soft fabric with slight gathers or tucks. Dressing in all one color slims just as well as wearing all black, which can be a bit of a bore after a while; a monochromatic dress under a bright blazer hides tummy bulges and a heavy bottom.

5. EASY CARE: FUSS-FREE FASHION

Who has the time or money to coddle hard-to-care-for duds? Not us! We try to take the easy route when we can: no-muss, no-fuss, no-worry that it will need to be ironed or dry-cleaned kind of clothing. I have two great looking dresses in particular that I love wearing because they follow all the rules of color, texture, and fit—*and* they're so easy to take care of. One is a sweater dress. I never have to worry that I'll have to iron it, or that it won't fall properly. And it looks great every time I wear it. My favorite is this easy-care lighter-weight knit dress. I can just machine wash, throw it in the dryer, and voila! It's clean! We're constantly on the road and these are the dresses I pack again and again. So, we advise you to have at least one or two the make-your-life-easy clothes in your closet.

On the other hand, there are clothes that are spectacular that aren't so easy to take care of. Our belly dance costumes are a good example of them. not that easy to take care of. Yet, of course, our closets are full of them! In a sense, we have two types of clothes—the easy-care ones and the high maintenance ones. The easy-care clothes are wrinkle-free and light, while the other is either a dry-cleaning or delicate hand-washable-dry-flat-type of clothing. Our costumes are all pretty high maintence. Some have light beading or coins and others heavier beading and fringe. So, if you don't have time to always go to the dry cleaners every time you wear your high-maintence clothes, try this tip we got from our wardrobe assistant. Mix two parts water and one part vodka and dab the mixture onto areas of the clothing to absorb any sweat or odor. On most fabrics, it works like a charm!

6. STAY FRESH: FASHION FUSION

Dressing for adornment is an ancient art form, but your outfits shouldn't look like a mummy's been wearing them! Although clothing can be traditional in style—or even retro—it should never look tired, old, or dated. Appearing to be at least somewhat in sync with the times sends a message of youthful energy and outlook, no matter what the occasion or your chronological age. In Egypt, Neena and I used to watch a few famous belly dancers, including Fifi Abdu, who always filled the house with people crazy to see what new costume she was wearing. She was a real trendsetter, and dressmakers would copy her latest efforts.

To stay fresh, special, attention getting, and on top of things, take a look at current magazines, TV shows, and movies to see what new twist they've come up with this season. The trick is to define your essential looks and then update them regularly to their current versions. Even that old standby, jeans, can't be worn forever; designers make subtle changes that make your five-year-old pair just look off and out of it.

One guaranteed way to keep your wardrobe looking fresh and spicy is to add a few exotic ethnic items. For example, take elements of a belly-dance costume—a beaded top or a flashy scarf—to spice up your image. Take the challenge to think creatively and go for fashion fusion.

One guaranteed way to keep your wardrobe looking fresh and spicy is to add a few exotic ethnic items. Take elements of a belly dance costume—a beaded top with jeans; a flashy scarf or even a belly dance hip scarf as a top—to spice up your image. Take the challenge to think outside the box—go for fashion fusion. For accessories, how about wearing earrings that are longer than what you normally would wear? Wear a bold color stone necklace to complement that mono color blouse.

Styles in India are especially exciting to us. They're always renewing their traditional styles with touches of Western design and attitude: They get ideas from the U.S., Americans get ideas from them, and as a result *everyone* looks more fabulous! So when you travel, be on the lookout for that special piece that you can't find anywhere else. When we're home in California, Neena likes to go to malls with mostly designer shops, and also frequents the small boutiques and independent designers. I'd rather bargain hunt and prefer to shop in downtown L.A.—I like to surprise myself with what I find, change up, and make alterations to.

Neena & Veena's Five Steps to Spice Up Your Wardrobe

Just as we transformed your kitchen and eating habits in Chapter 2, we're going to give your closet and dressing habits a makeover. We've divided our program into five steps. The first part involves research and planning, and then we'll look at four types of clothes: workout/casual wear, everyday/career attire, lingerie, and special occasion/night-on-the-town apparel. For each type, we'll help you go through your closet and empty out the losers: clothes that don't make you feel or look good. Then we'll show you how to go shopping and fill your closet with winners: things that make you feel good and look great!

Unlike the food makeover, though, we won't put a time frame on these steps for a couple of reasons: First, you may be on a weight-loss program, so it would be silly to buy a bunch of new clothes that soon will be too large; or to toss out "thin" clothes from another life that don't fit you now—but that might be perfectly fine for the new you. Second, money may be an issue, so you'll need to determine your budget first. From there, you can figure out a schedule for your clothing expenses.

When tossing, shopping, and experimenting with your clothes, go with your gut instinct as you pick your styles: Be bold, be brave, and be creative! Try to get someone you trust to be your first audience member. (I'm pretty lucky, because I just use Neena!) Maybe you can swap services with a friend or sister—be each other's critics and fashion consultants, the way my sister and I are for each other. Even one or two salespeople are better than no one. If you're really clueless and so are your friends and family, there's nothing wrong with hiring a professional wardrobe consultant.

Throughout the rest of the chapter, we'll talk about getting rid of some things and making new acquisitions. Here are some tips to keep in mind as you go along:

— **Tossing:** When going through your closets, make it fun—you can play dance music and have a fashion show. My sister and I have done that a lot, especially when we lived together. Try on everything in each clothing category and judge it as to color, texture, fit, flattering cut, and freshness.

How long has it been since you've worn the item? If it's been two or more years . . . out it goes. (One of my neighbors says that she tosses something if she hasn't worn it in six months!) Do you avoid a particular item because it's too expensive to keep clean? Ding! Use it or lose it!

Literally toss the losers into three piles: sell, give away to charity, and throw away. I promise that this feels really good—in fact, Neena and I do this often. You need to clear out the old to make way for the new and fabulous stuff to come. You'll have more room for the clothes you keep—and they won't look so wrinkled either! In addition, you'll no longer spend time desperately getting dressed, trying to make something work that was doomed from the start.

It's fine to keep clothing that's no longer in style if you update it by making alterations. When we were growing up, Neena and I used to alter the clothes we bought in thrift shops or that were handed down to us; some were almost totally reconstructed. We did this both out of the need to save money *and* because we really enjoyed it: It got our creative juices flowing! One way to update your jeans, for instance, is to sew fun stuff on them. (One of my favorite pairs of jeans, which gets a lot of compliments, is full of sequins on the front.) This look can be elegant, playful, or funky, depending on your individual style.

If you want to rescue clothes this way, my advice is that you'd better give yourself a deadline! Don't *plan* on doing it "someday," and don't *save* it for a rainy day. Pull out your calendar and make the "reconstruction" commitment date—otherwise, it may never get done. Also, remember to be realistic about the item's condition: Watch for tears, stains, or tattered material. I remember when Neena revamped a shirt that she loved. It was a true overhaul: She changed the sleeves, tapered the bodice, and fixed the neckline. It looked way different and really cool. The problem was that the material had formed "pills"—those horrible little balls from old material—and I insisted that she get rid of it. Oh well, it was good practice for her sewing skills!

— **Shopping:** This is the time to experiment and be open-minded about trying things that you wouldn't ordinarily consider. Who cares if the color or fabric ends up being wrong? You have nothing to lose, and you're gaining experience, ideas, and the ability to look at yourself in a different light. But *do* be discriminating about what makes it with you to the checkout counter.

Always try the clothes on in the store first and look at yourself in a full-length mirror. Once you're in the dressing room, your new rule is: If you don't love it, you don't buy it. "Okay" isn't good enough! And "a fabulous bargain" is still a money pit if you won't wear it.

It's interesting how a dress can look amazing on a hanger, but not so great once it's on. The color might be right, but the style and fit could be all wrong, or vice versa. But I've also found shirts or pants that were just okay on the rack, but my belly told me: "Try it on—you never know!" And they turned out to be sooooo cute!

I almost always ask a salesperson for help, since they usually know what's on the racks; and especially in small shops, they're also likely to know what clothing to pull out for specific types of customers. Also, find out what the store's return policy is. If they won't allow you to take anything back (as many boutiques won't), be sure to select what you absolutely love and can afford. Use your belly feeling to decide on all your purchases—it's easier on your bank account!

Okay girlfriend, now that you have these tips, let's get busy. . . .

Step 1: Get Ready

▨ Immerse yourself in the sensual world of color, texture, and design.
▨ Research and plan how you're going to stock your own at-home boutique.

This is like having a party and doing your homework all at the same time! What we want you to do is think about the basic principles outlined earlier: color, texture, fit, and so on. What kinds of clothes look and feel good on you? Which pieces that you own (or used to own) got complimented every time they saw the light of day, and which ones did you wear until they fell apart? What was it about these garments that worked so well?

After you've answered these questions, go window-shopping for ideas. Browse at different shops, from small boutiques to department stores. Look at mannequins, watch TV with an eye for the clothing, read magazines and catalogs, and visit fabric stores to see which colors, textures, styles, and prints appeal to you. Neena and I make regular trips to the fashion and fabric districts in downtown L.A. Many of these places also sell fun beads, fabric glitter, sequins, and appliqués that are great for glitzing up and accessorizing any wardrobe. (We do this a lot with our belly-dance costumes.) There are so many different kinds of shops now, and they can be a source of ideas and inspiration whether or not you're into sewing.

Next, think about a time frame for your clothing transformation: Maybe you need to go the gradual route, discarding and replacing things slowly; or perhaps you're able to do a big "purge and splurge." So decide on a

budget, planning how much you can spend and over what period of time. We both like to buy clothes of good quality, since they last longer, look better, and we're worth it—and so are you! But there's also part of me that loves bargains. While Neena would rather spend $100 to $200 on one gorgeous, high-quality sweater (instead of spreading that same amount over several sweaters), I like to buy stuff that just *looks* like I spent a fortune on it. All I do is apply one of our belly-makeover techniques, such as taper or accessorize . . . and voilà! It's a whole new outfit!

Don't get me wrong: I'm not being cheap. Instead, it's kind of like a game to me. Sometimes I'll wear an outfit and say to Neena, "Hey, guess how much this cost me!" Okay, so I like gloating! It's all in fun (but really, who *doesn't* like a bargain?). If you're really on a tight budget and you don't sew, then you might want to look at only sales or outlets. Some of my favorite dresses and shirts were on the clearance racks: I had a $10 dress that I wore a lot, and I did nothing to it!

Sometimes you can also get great deals on used clothing in secondhand shops, thrift stores, church sales, swap meets, the Internet, and consignment shops. Often the clothing has been worn only once or twice—or not at all! When my sister and I were kids, we wore used clothing half the time because our family couldn't always afford the new stuff. Today, we still might go secondhand if we need a special item for a particular performance. Or maybe retro is your thing. These styles look great on some people, and the fabric and craftsmanship are often better than what's available in contemporary clothing.

If you're following a weight-loss or fitness plan and expect your body shape and size to change, you'll stay in this planning and dreaming stage for a while. Depending on your finances, you might want to buy some inexpensive in-between clothes that fit your changing body; you might also see what secondhand stores have to offer.

Now that we have you drooling over the possibilities and raring to go, you're ready to tackle the next step. . . .

STEP 2: WORKOUT AND CASUAL-WEAR MAKEOVER

※ Go through the things you wear for exercising and playtime; and toss those that are outdated, worn, ill-fitting, unstylish, or unbecoming.

※ Shop for workout and casual clothes that are right for you—and right for *now*.

We start our makeover here because if you have workout clothes that you enjoy, you're more likely to actually get some exercise! These days, casual wear and fitness gear have so much in common that many of these pieces can do double duty. Cool tank tops, stretch pants, and hoodies can all be fashionable yet comfortable, go from one occasion to another, and allow you to always be ready to dance.

Many women—especially if they're overweight or unaccustomed to exercise— gravitate toward very big, loose, and unflattering sweatshirts and baggy sweatpants. Even though these are comfortable, they have too much bulk for dancing—and they sure don't make you feel like a sexy belly dancer—so toss them! And chuck anything else that's the wrong color for you or that feels uncomfortable or unsexy. Do you wear ancient leggings with stretched-out elastic? Out! That sad T-shirt with a peeling college logo on it—out!

No matter what form of exercise you prefer, get yourself decked out as if you were going to a belly-dance class. What I mean is that you should wear something cool and flattering that lets you enjoy and experience movement. Neena and I saw a woman speed-walking with a group of friends in cool weather: She was wearing simple, fitted navy sweats, but she accessorized with bright-red-velvet gloves and a flash of matching red lipstick. She looked fabulous!

And, if you *are* taking belly-dance classes or using a tape or DVD at home, why not dress the part? A flowing skirt, leggings, harem pants, *choli* (see page 108), crop top, sports bra, fitted T-shirt, tank top, or camisole . . . any of these will make your workout more enjoyable and more authentic feeling. A hip scarf or any fun, colorful fabric that you may have at home that's tied around your hips—or coin-decorated hoop earrings—help create a belly-dance effect with any fitness wear.

For casual occasions, I might wear cute and trendy tracksuits for comfort, dressing them up with earrings or a bracelet, and maybe accenting them with a matching hairband or hat. There's nothing wrong with wearing comfy clothes if they're flattering in color and fit, and if you accessorize them so that you look more attractive. Use your own imagination to make your most casual outfits memorable.

Comfy doesn't have to mean lazy and uncaring. If you wear jeans, make sure that they're stylish, updated, and fit great. The fabric has gotten thinner recently—more supple and sensual—and I love the ones that have some spandex in them for a clingy fit with lots of comfort.

These days, there are many different styles for *all* body types. You can pick where you want the fit to be: classic cut, hip-huggers, just below the waist, low-rise, or super low-rise for the daring woman! Choices at the hem include: boot cut, flared, tapered, and straight legged. Pair your favorites with a stylish top for casual dancing and parties . . . and you're set!

It's such fun to incorporate a bit of the belly-dance look, too—a bra top with a button-down shirt tied over it or a maybe a cute, fitted blazer; or an Indian choli with jeans, a skirt, or even dressy pants. We've worn this look to great effect at press parties and during TV appearances. Some belly dancers wear flexible, sparkly flat shoes for performing, and these translate well into a unique look. You can also have lots of fun with a hip scarf: We've made tops out of them and worn them with simple skirts or jeans. Just bring the wide ends of the triangle to your back and tie them together, letting the tip of the triangle hang down to partially cover your midriff for a peekaboo effect. Or, of course, you could tie it around your hips over your jeans or skirt to accentuate your hips and movement, belly-dance style. Sometimes I even tie a veil or a coined chain from Afghanistan through the belt loops of my jeans.

STEP 3: CAREER-CLOTHES MAKEOVER

* As you did with your workout and casual garments, go through what you wear for work and toss anything that's outdated, worn, ill-fitting, unstylish, or unbecoming.

* Shop for career clothes that are right for you—and right for *now*.

Now it's time to tackle the working part of your wardrobe. You probably spend most of your life in these clothes—shouldn't they give you pleasure as well as get the job done? So whether you wear a uniform or casual attire to the office, you don't have to ignore your sensuality and femininity. So what's a worker bee with a belly-dance attitude to do?

If it's any consolation, my sister and I also face certain limitations. I've already mentioned how crucial it is for our stage costumes to fit perfectly. But we also need to pay attention to the clothes we wear when we show up at our gigs, before we even get onto the stage. Because Neena and I are businesswomen, we have to be practical, too. We need to look professional and presentable, and of course feel comfortable—but without looking dumpy. I choose to wear comfortable but snug dresses, because pants or anything with a belt or elastic that binds at my waist will leave temporary lines on my belly area (like pillowcase lines on your face in the morning), and when I change into my costume, everyone can see those marks!

Overcome *your* work-clothes realities by creatively expressing yourself in subtle ways. Put a sensual silk blouse in a flattering color under your suit jacket, and wear bigger or even slightly funky earrings or other jewelry to spice up an otherwise conservative outfit.

You might need to wear heels at certain times. Again, fit is key since even high heels can be more comfortable if they're good-quality shoes in the right size and width, or if you put a thin pad of cushioning at the ball of the foot. Maybe you don't *really* need to wear those styles at all—will a lower or chunky style be acceptable?

Depending on your circumstances, see if you can gently push the envelope in other ways. It's definitely worth the effort to increase your happiness with your work costume—you'll do a better job! And now that you've gotten the hang of how to accomplish your career-clothes makeover, get your creativity in high gear and save up your bucks for the next step. . . .

STEP 4: UNDER-YOUR-CLOTHES MAKEOVER

✳ Go through your underwear and bra drawers and toss any ill-fitting or nonmatching undergarments.

✳ Shop for lingerie that's right for you—and right for *now*.

How can a girl feel sexy if she's wearing loose underwear or a bra with overly stretched elastic? Even if people can't (or may not) see those panty lines, *you* know they're there—and you owe it to yourself to feel good.

You need sensual and sexy lingerie, so how about buying yourself a strappy teddy and matching G-string or a lace bra with a thong? Maybe you could try a sexy bustier, merry widow, or gown. If you're sticking to just bras and panties, buy matching black lacy pieces . . . or strapless nude. Here's something else to consider: push-up bras or pads. It doesn't hurt to get a little help once in a while; belly-dance costumes often have padding up top to create a little cleavage—sexy!

Neena likes wearing underwear that matches her clothes in color, texture, and mood. If she's sporting casual cotton clothes, she'll wear cotton underthings; if she's wearing silk on the outside, silk goes on the bottom layer, too. And my choices absolutely affect how I feel, carry myself, and move. My sister and I don't care if anyone else sees these things—that's not the point. We're fulfilling our belief about sensuality: It starts from the inside.

For an extra luxurious feeling, spray your lingerie drawer with your favorite scent every now and then. No one else may know, but you'll smile every time you open it. Whether you wear these naughty scraps under your clothes or under the covers, this is one sure, sensual way to feel good about yourself. While you're at it, you can wear your lingerie to show off those undulations!

STEP 5: "NIGHT-ON-THE-TOWN" CLOTHES MAKEOVER

✳ As you did with your casual and career clothes, sort through what you wear for going out and on special occasions and toss those that are outdated, worn, ill-fitting, unstylish, and unbecoming.

✳ Shop for night-on-the-town clothes that are right for you—and right for *now*.

This is the place where you can really shine—literally and figuratively. Go for the glitz, the glitter, the colors, the most sensual fabrics, and the sexiest styles: It's playtime! From romantic, intimate dinners to dancing, parties, and the hottest clubs, here's where you can be as simple and elegant or outrageously flamboyant as your taste and pocketbook allow. All of life is a stage, but when you're on the dance floor or making your entrance at a fancy affair or special restaurant, you want your costume to draw more attention to you than at any other times in your life.

Let's be honest: Belly-dance outfits are sensual and sexy. They're a tried-and-true combination of revealing and covering up, with a seductive, cleavage-enhancing beaded bra on top, sensually swaying chiffon fabric below, and hips set off with a jeweled belt. Unless you're giving a performance, you won't want to wear the whole outfit, but you can certainly duplicate its effects. Bare skin is hot—whether it's your belly, back, legs, cleavage, or shoulders and arms.

Belly dancers know how to create a seductive, attractive, and slightly mysterious effect with a low-riding skirt or harem pants, which are often slit to reveal glimpses of leg. Sometimes just a little peekaboo lace or see-through fabric can be a turn-on, since the less you see, the hotter you look. A dress that covers your arms and legs— but reveals a sensuous back or provocative cleavage—is hot hot hot! So be a little mysterious . . . or a lot.

In Egypt, female belly dancers must cover up their bellies. They wear nude netting over their midriffs so that it still looks as though they're wearing a two-piece costume, but they're technically covered up. Apply this principle to your own clothes—that is, if you choose to cover up your belly or any other part of your anatomy, there are still ways to make it look sexy. Black netting has a wonderful teasing quality, and there are lots of sheer fabrics that you can use to cover an area while still hinting at its sensuality.

Then there's the veil—what a fantastic ancient invention! When all you can see of a dancer is her eyes, there's tantalizing anticipation of seeing bare skin when the veil gets dropped or set aside, even if it's just her arms and face. We're all dying to know what's behind the veil, and we've heard guys say the same thing: If you're showing everything, there's no mystery, no challenge. So you don't necessarily need to bare a lot of skin.

Zills 'n Thrills: Belly-Dance Costumes

Belly-dance costumes are the essence of sensuality and pizzazz, and there's quite a variety of clothing and styles to choose from. The typical clothing really shows your curves, but a bare belly isn't mandatory—or even traditional! (The two-piece bra-and-belt outfit that's now considered "traditional" was actually invented in Hollywood movies.) It's all relative . . . you might feel sexy in something low cut or that bares your midriff. Or maybe you'd be more comfortable and confident in a costume that covers the torso, which can be just as sexy and alluring, especially when it's made of semisheer fabric or some kind of netting.

Just as there are different styles of belly dance, there are various kinds of costumes. Although fashions are always changing, here are some general notes:

- **Turkish** style is known for its sequins and harem pants. The belts are usually triangular.
- **Cabaret** style is usually the most glamorous and ornate.
- **Egyptian** style usually has beaded fringes.
- **American Tribal,** based on a fusion of many traditions, includes an ornate headpiece, choli, many fabric layers, and lots of antique jewelry.

Costume Components

— **Bra:** Not your everyday bra—or even a Wonderbra—these are weighty and substantial because they're heavily decorated with beads, sequins, or coins. Some have fringe, beads, coins, or tassels hanging down to draw your eye to the torso and belly, or fringe or epaulets at the shoulders to accentuate those shimmies.

— **Choli top:** Of Indian origin, this snug-fitting, short-sleeved, cropped top may be decorated along the hem with coins, beads, sequins, and the like. Usually worn by American Tribal belly dancers, some women feel more comfortable in this more-subdued top.

— **Hip belt:** The classic belt fits snugly around the hips, exposing the midriff so that undulations and belly rolls are visible. It matches the sequins, beads, or jewels of the bra, and may also have tassels, coins, or fringe hanging down to emphasize your hip movements.

— **Skirt:** Skirts are usually made of layered circles of chiffon or other floaty fabric, or may be a blunt straight cut. Although they cover you down to the ground, many have slits that allow the legs to move and peek through.

— **Harem pants:** Full-cut of lightweight fabric (such as chiffon or gauze) and gathered at the ankle, harem pants are an alternative to skirts.

— **Beledi dress:** This full-length belly-dance dress usually covers the midriff with fabric that might be sheer and formfitting. Many times the skirt is slit provocatively up to the thigh.

— **Veils:** These are a great way to add mystery and playfulness to your belly dance. They come in many colors and fabrics that usually match the skirt (or harem pants) and/or the bra and belt. Used for a grand entrance among Egyptian dancers, veils have emerged in the last 100 years as a favorite among American and other Western belly dancers, but are rarely used in the actual dancing in Middle Eastern nightclubs.

— **Arm and head accessories:** Embellish to the max with fingerless gloves called "gauntlets"; wrist cuffs; bracelets; arm-, neck-, and headbands; and turbans or other headdresses. Arm cuffs in gold or other materials are a tradition in North Africa.

— **Finger cymbals:** Four small brass discs that you hear and see played by dancers. One on each thumb and middle finger to incorporate and accentuate different rhythmic patterns into the dance. Finger cymbals date back to 200 B.C.E. Here's what they're called in four different languages:

- ❊ *Zills:* Turkish
- ❊ *Sagat* or *sunouj:* Arabic
- ❊ *Zang:* Persian
- ❊ *Manjira* or *manzira:* East Indian

While you may not want to walk around wearing finger cymbals outside of a belly-dance class, you can translate their flirty sounds into some over-the-top, attention-grabbing ethnic earrings, pendants, or coin-bedecked necklaces and bracelets (called *sawar* in Tunisia). Or how about some tinkly ankle bracelets (called *redif* in Morocco)? American Tribal belly dancers have made wearing elaborate antique jewelry part of their distinctive style. If it suits your look, why not make it *your* signature as well?

— **Hip scarves:** Hip scarves are a delight to wear and watch, accentuating your movements and enhancing your performance or workout. Use a sash or scarf that you already own, or get one with gold-colored coins. The shimmer and tinkling sound of the metal are an integral part of belly dance and will transport you magically to another land.

But wait, there's more: Other accessories that you'll see belly dancers using and that you might like to try are swords, canes, and snakes. (Just kidding!)

111

Fit, as always, is important—and not everything needs to be tight. Sometimes looser clothing, if it drapes sensually and clings to your womanly curves, can also be an incredible turn-on. Few men can resist a sheer, feminine floral dress in touchable fabric that floats around your body. One belly dancer friend of ours feels sexiest when she wears layers of gossamer scarves over her loose sheer harem pants. Everything is very flowing and creates a unique look and feel. If that's your idea of sexy, and you can project your charisma this way, then it *is* sexy! After all, being comfortable in your skin and the confidence that exudes is very attractive.

And don't forget texture: The feel of your clothes can make or break a date for you *and* your companion. If you wear something stiff and scratchy—no matter how spectacular—you'll be miserable, and your companion won't want to touch you either. It's not much fun for anybody if you can't wait to get home and *get out* of those itchy things . . . well, actually, that part could be interesting. . . .

Speaking of which, what's underneath *does* count, so don't forget to buy beautiful, sexy lingerie for those special nights. If you feel sensual inside because you're wearing lovely lace (or satin or silk) on the outside, maybe that special someone will see it and respond in a pleasantly surprising new way.

There are even more simple steps that can project a more low-key sensuality, exoticness, and availability. Even if you just tie a belly-dance scarf around your hips, suddenly everything looks more fashionable. It really puts you in the mood and turns you into an instant belly dancer! If you don't have a belly-dance hip scarf, any bright scarf will do. Many of our colleagues adorn their heads with something flashy, and Neena and I have wrapped our veils around our hair for a chic, trendsetting look. For an "in vogue" night out, we've also taken a veil and threaded it through the belt loops of our jeans, and worn this with a matching belly-dance top.

I like the fun vibe of my pink pants made of silky sari fabric. They have turquoise trim, and I often top them off with a turquoise ethnic-looking top. You could also couple that top with a simple solid color, like a black or white skirt or pair of pants, and embellish the look with pink and turquoise bracelets to tie it all together for a swanky Indian look.

Another way to sizzle it up for a night on the town is to wear animal prints, which send a subliminal message of primal attraction . . . grrrrr. No matter what your age or body type, you can find something that announces your inner wild beast, such as eyeglass frames, shoes, or a belt in a leopard or snake print (faux, of course!) All the better if you're an animal lover like my sister and I are—it pays to advertise!

Dress-up shoes can be a problem or a pleasure. Heels elevate any outfit—even jeans—to a different level, but they can be the most uncomfortable thing you're wearing. A good solution is to try ballroom-dance shoes, which look sexier than flats or sensible low heels. Since they're made for dancing, they provide flexibility and support and are quite comfortable. I have a pair in silver and one in gold. We not only use these professionally, but I actually sometimes wear them to go out! And they are way more comfortable than most other heels. Flat shoes can be sexy, too—if they have thin straps that crisscross up the ankle, a gold or other flashy metallic finish, or trim that catches the eye (such as bangles or beads).

For really special occasions, though, you might want to spring for a pair of "limo shoes"—you know, the kind that are strictly for showing off. I wear them if I know I'm going to be sitting a lot. They can be excruciating when you wear them for long periods of time—but they're so much fun to look at!

Getting Dressed Is Half the Fun

Now that you've got the clothes, let's get them out of the closet and put them onto your body. Why not extend the adventure and have some fun before you even go out the door? Throw some music on your stereo or turn on your iPod, and pick something that makes you feel the way you want to when you're going out. Got a hot, romantic date? Play something soft, sensual, and sexy, and burn a little incense to set the mood. If you're stepping out to a big, loud party, play dance music full blast—it'll really rev up your energy.

The right tunes will bring out the emotions that you'll be feeling at the occasion, and you'll get a feeling for the right colors and style, so you'll be more likely to choose just the right outfit. It's as if you're warming up for a performance by doing a little belly dance to get in the groove for moving and holding your body in a new way. The same holds true for these other occasions. Getting ready for a big presentation at work? Perhaps a little Wagner will set the right tone. For a casual get-together with friends, relax with something mellow, such as an oud taksim. When you surround yourself with music, you'll literally start walking to a different beat and get in sync with your outfit from the inside out.

All Dressed Up and Someplace to Go

From working out to hanging out . . . from the office to a hot date, your clothes are sending a message to the world. Now you know how to control that message and shape it to be whatever you want! A clothing makeover is an easy, quick way to access your inner belly dancer and broadcast the sensual, confident, strong, unique, expressive inner you. Wearing the right outfit is guaranteed to improve your ability to perform on any stage—and at any life stage.

You're almost ready for your debut performance! There's just one more step to go: Let's put your best face forward.

✳ ✳ ✳ ✳ ✳ ✳

Chapter Seven

BEAUTIFY YOUR BELLY . . .
ENHANCING YOUR BEST FEATURES
BY NEENA

As far back as I can remember, Veena and I have been as fascinated by makeup as we have been by clothes—they went hand in hand. Our mother wasn't a belly dancer by a long shot (she was a grade-school teacher), but she liked to look good and knew how important it was to embellish her face, whether it was for work, social occasions, or grocery shopping.

In India, it's traditional for women to use a black-powder eyeliner called *surma* or *kajol* (also known as *kohl* in Arabic-speaking countries); these days, this product also comes in a cream base. Our mom followed this ancient tradition when we were growing up: I remember being mesmerized as she took her surma stick and in two deft strokes accented her eyes with a dark, smoky halo, just as millions of Indian women had done before her. It looked so quick and easy!

Well, it wasn't easy for *me*—at least not in the beginning. I was seven years old when I first tried to put it on myself, which turned out to be a little painful and messy. I poked myself in the eye and the powder was all over my face, so I looked like a raccoon by the time I was finished! I found out the hard way that it takes a steady hand to apply a clean line from one corner of the eye to the other.

Surma was the first makeup that Veena and I used. We thought it made us look like Indian film stars, and our mom didn't mind. Eye makeup on Indian girls isn't the big-deal rite of passage that it is in Western countries. In fact, Mom used to put it on us when we were around two years old because it was just part of the custom. When we got a bit older, I remember seeing our baby-girl cousins with dark lines around their eyes.

When I asked my aunt why they had it on, she said, "It's made of herbs, so it nourishes and protects—and it's very expressive." That's when I realized that in our culture, the eyes are probably the most important facial features because they're the real communicators, especially in dance and onstage.

My love of cosmetics didn't end with surma: Mom was also into lipsticks, red nail polish, and moisturizing creams. Veena experimented with the polish by applying it to her lips—she wanted the permanent effect since Mom's lipstick would smudge off if she kissed us. But she found out pretty fast that polish isn't very kissable!

We also used to watch our mother put moisturizer on her face. I started experimenting with products such as petroleum jelly and vitamin-E oil by putting a little on my eyebrows to "train" them into a shape that I liked, some on my lashes to emphasize them, and a smudge on my lips for gloss. My sister and I played with our mother's creams and lotions, pretending that we were doing TV commercials in the mirror. We'd take each cosmetic, apply it to our face before the "camera," and explain why it was good: "This makes you skin so soft . . . try it and see. . . ." Little did we know that one day we'd be making commercials for real!

Today we still have lots of creative fun with our exotic paint boxes. Embellishing your face, hair, and hands—and maybe even your belly—is an easy, relatively inexpensive way to explore your outer beauty and express your inner self. The modern versions of the ancient art of cosmetics (which includes makeup, hair color, nail polish, and body decorations) can enhance what you've got and help you be whomever you want to be. From natural to artificial to elegant to edgy, you can choose the look you want to have at any moment.

Choosing Your Look

Your makeup can be as unique and expressive as your clothing. So begin by taking a look at your face, hair, and hands in the mirror to determine your strengths, as well as those features that you'd rather not shine the spotlight on. Maybe there's something you never particularly cared for that could become an asset if you play it right because it shows off your individuality.

For example, when I was a teen, I didn't like my "ethnic" look of heavy brows and prominent nose and lips; I wanted to be blonde with thin lips. Today, strong noses, heavy eyebrows, almond-shaped eyes, and tightly curled hair are not only totally acceptable, they're desirable to many people. So whatever your look is, play it up—don't cover it up! It's your unique image and identity. Nowadays, you'll see all kinds of different looks and ethnicities in magazines and on billboards.

Whether or not you have a so-called ethnic heritage, you can adopt some aspects of any look you like by using new cosmetics—or using familiar ones in new ways. The tradition of ancient Egypt, Persia, and India was always to emphasize the eyes. And if you've ever seen historic paintings from those regions, you'll notice that even hundreds of years ago, it was common to draw black lines around women's eyes. My Indian classical-dance teacher also told me once that temple dancers used their eyes to express emotion and tell the stories of the gods to the audience from a distance, and that kajol framed the eyes, which are just as important as arm and body movements. Veena and I took this look and integrated it into a modern, Westernized style to complement our costumes and define our own image.

Even though Western fashion goes back and forth between emphasizing the eyes and focusing on the lips, I still think that the eyes are the most important. Big or small, wide set or close together, deep brown or clear emerald green, they're the most expressive part of your face, and there are so many colors and tricks that you can use to make them look more prominent. While the smoky dark-hued look isn't for everybody, it *may* be for you (at least for certain occasions). So try it—you may be pleasantly surprised!

When choosing your unique look, you don't have to pick just one. In fact, Veena and I encourage you to have several "faces," depending on your mood and your intended audience. Are you headed for a workout? Then you probably want to go without makeup or keep it to a bare minimum—just a few strokes of waterproof mascara and a touch of understated lipstick or tinted gloss. If you're hanging out with friends, then take it to the next level: Maybe add eyebrow pencil and a little eyeliner for further definition. Off to a regular day at the office? Take it up another notch with foundation and blush for a professional look. And if you'll be going out on a hot date, dancing in a club, attending a big party, or having some other type of big night, you'll want your makeup to be equal in intensity to your fabulous costume.

We belly dancers need to pump up the volume to keep pace with our brightly colored, beaded costumes that catch the eye and sparkle in the spotlight. We'd look absolutely washed out if we didn't get our faces, hair, and nails on the same wavelength as our clothes.

This same rule is followed all over the world, in every circumstance. In India, for example, where women wear colorful clothes every day and also go heavy on the jewelry, they instinctively balance this effect with lots of surma so that their beautiful, expressive faces don't disappear. The same is true for the women in many North African and Middle Eastern countries. So, just as you make sure that your outfit is appropriate for the occasion, get used to choosing the intensity and style of your cosmetics to coordinate the entire look.

To balance this out, make sure that the amount of makeup you're wearing is at a level where you're comfortable—not overblown, self-conscious, or unflattering—since you still want to express who you are. This just may be an opportunity to explore a side of you that doesn't often get to show itself, so have fun with it!

Now's the time to pull out your new clothes so that you can coordinate them with your face. Take stock of your current style: If you've been wearing the same kind of makeup for years, or if you wear little or nothing on your face and are tired of fading into the background all the time, it's time for a change. In this chapter, I'll give you a step-by step program to help you beautify, decorate, and transform your face, hair, and nails for any occasion. But first, a few basic principles.

Look Amazing: The Basics

Belly beauty is *total* beauty—and that means dealing with the inside as well as the outside. I love what cosmetics can do, but the most important treatments I can recommend don't have anything to do with eye shadow and lipstick. Your skin, hair, and nails all originate inside of you; as they grow and emerge, they become your inner self made visible on the surface, reflecting what's going on within your body and mind. That's why healthy habits show up as clear, glowing, smooth skin; shiny hair; and strong, flexible nails. (Great sex is beautifying, too, 'cause it puts that sparkle in your eye and a smile on your lips!) So keep these tips in mind—and pretty soon you may be turning down offers to do cosmetic, shampoo, and nail-polish commercials!

— **Take care of your insides.** Exercise brings more oxygen and nutrients to your skin so that it's firmer and better nourished; eating fresh foods and drinking lots of water help, too. My mom always told Veena and me to try to stay away from "dead food"—that is, items that are canned, frozen, or dried. Instead, she encouraged us to eat lots of raw fruits and veggies and nuts; and to drink plenty of water, which not only hydrates the body, but also keeps the hair and nails in good condition.

— **Let go of stress.** Tension can show up on your face, no matter how well you take care of your skin. Stress can mess with your hormones and lead to dull, dry hair—and even hair loss! So do something relaxing that you enjoy every day, whether it's going for a walk, or taking time to belly dance, or just vegging out!

— **Pamper your skin, hair, and nails regularly.** Take care of your skin every day. For example, don't go to bed wearing makeup, since cosmetics left on overnight seep into your pores, clog them, and congest your skin. For an extra-clean, nourished complexion, exfoliate and use facial masks regularly, along with moisturizing morning and evening. Take care of your cuticles by working in cuticle cream at night.

Living in Southern California or visiting countries such as Egypt or India, the dry weather can be especially hard on the skin, so Veena and I make sure to hydrate our faces frequently throughout the day. I like to make an effective hydrator by filling a spray bottle with distilled water and adding a few drops of rose essential oil; shake it gently before spraying on, even over makeup—another ancient Middle Eastern and Indian beauty secret!

— **Treat yourself gently.** Never pull, tug, or scrub your delicate facial skin, and be very gentle when you cleanse, moisturize, and put on makeup—this will lessen the chance that you'll damage your skin and cause wrinkles. Protect your hands and nails from water with latex gloves, and prevent injury by wearing work gloves

in the garden and when doing chores. Choose comfortable, properly fitting shoes as often as possible so that you don't get corns and scrunched-up toes.

— **Protect yourself.** Keep sun exposure to a minimum, and wear a wide-brimmed hat or sunscreen when you're outdoors. As we mentioned before, in the Middle East and India, veils are often used to protect skin from the sun, desert sands, wind, and other harsh elements. I like to wear a light-cotton long-sleeved *kamiz* (Middle Eastern–style blouse) or shirt for protection, or a sleeveless shirt with nongreasy natural sunscreen; while shea butter is Veena's favorite. Many foundations and moisturizers also contain sunscreen, which is great. If you prefer a tanned look, you may want to get a safe golden glow with self-tanner or bronzer.

Winter months or living in a dry climate can often mean that the air in your home contains little moisture. To keep skin supple and hair shiny and static-free, invest in a humidifier or place bowls of water around your home.

Getting Started

Once you've got the basics, you're ready to embark on the belly way, which will inspire you to try new things and realize that cosmetics can transform you from head to toe into the most attractive, sensual, feminine being possible. But in order to move forward, you've got to be bold enough to break out of your old habits, just like the kid I used to be, who was fascinated with cosmetics.

Think more like a child, discovering a colorful, magical world. Open your eyes and mind to new looks, colors, products, and ways of applying cosmetics. Experiment and get caught up in the moment!

Begin by studying the makeup on other women's faces in magazines, TV shows, and movies . . . or maybe even at your friends' homes. Just look and observe. Another way to become familiar with the endless possibilities of colors for your face is to pay a visit to a makeup counter in a department or cosmetics store. See what the women there are wearing—both customers and employees. For more fun (and moral support!), bring a trusted, creative friend with you.

It's playtime, so use those testers—that's what they're there for! Pretend you're a kid in a toy store . . . or an artist in a paint store . . . and you're the canvas. Wow—look at all the colors! This is the time to try things that you wouldn't ordinarily think of wearing. Salespeople will be more than happy to help you find the next great thing, and if there's a trained consultant at the counter, all the better.

Makeup is usually sectioned off by brand names, not just by categories, but feel free to mix and match—brand loyalty isn't required! (You may like one brand of foundation, but a different mascara.) If you ask for a makeover, the consultants will gladly give you one. These are usually free and, although each salesperson's training and experience will vary, you'll always get fresh ideas to try out.

Be open to what might seem like wild suggestions—they might be on to something! Eye makeup in particular is surprising: Colors you wouldn't think would work together can somehow look stylish. I've usually been happy with the results when I've had makeovers, because how a certain makeup artist saw my face gave me insight and inspiration to get a little bolder with on my own application afterward.

Even slightly jazzing up or changing your current everyday look creates a bold statement. You can still be natural without appearing drab (which just makes you feel boring). Even a new lipstick color that you never would have thought to use can change your whole look and even energize your mood.

Veena and I have also gotten our faces done by many different makeup artists at our various gigs, photo shoots, and television shows. We're always getting new ideas from them and being excited by new people with fresh perspectives. On the other hand, there have been some clunkers—thank God for makeup remover! They may be experts, but they don't know your personality or your belly essence. *You* know yourself and your face better than anyone else. Remember: You need to like and be comfortable with the results. Your face should still be recognizable—but maybe just a different version that beautifully enhances your qualities and gifts!

The point is to have fun with cosmetics, and the beauty is that they're a temporary art. The stuff scrubs off, washes out, and grows out, so you can always start the experiment all over again. Don't be timid or limit yourself at this point . . . how creative can you be in getting the effect you want?

Give Your Makeup Kit a Makeover

Veena and I have come a long way since our early days of surma and petroleum jelly. We love trying out new products, and now that you're in the makeup mode, it's time for you to do a bit of shopping, too. While you may want to experiment with what you have on hand, don't stop there! We recommend buying some "toys" (see our list of essentials below) and then playing with them at home. Just remember, nothing lasts forever: It's recommended that you at least replace your eye makeup every three to six months to avoid possible infection.

Have all the fun you want with testers in the store, but when it comes to plunking down actual cash, buy wisely. Many cosmetics counters have samples or travel sizes for you to try, and I've found that you have to test different products to see which ones work for you. Don't be influenced by the price—that is, just because it's expensive doesn't mean that it's good or it lasts; and if it's cheap, the quality can still be there or the product might really work well.

Just keep trying various brands until you find something that works well for you. Also, realize that colors look different under various conditions. The fluorescent lighting in the store may be similar to that at your workplace, but how will you look outdoors? When I test a new product or shade, I sometimes go outside and take a mirror with me to see what the color and texture will look like there.

With all of that in mind, here's a suggested shopping list (keep reading for more information about each one of these items):

- Base foundation
- Contouring foundation
- Concealer
- Blush
- Powder
- Eye shadows
- Eyeliner
- Mascara
- Eyebrow pencil (and/or powder)
- Lip pencil
- Lipstick or lip gloss
- Brushes
- Q-tips
- Sponges
- Shimmering bronze tint or body glitter

NEENA & VEENA'S GETAWAY KIT

During Veena's first year in college, she kept just two cosmetics in her bag: a kohl-like pencil for her eyes and a tinted lip gloss. Although her selection has grown (quite a bit!) since then, she still feels that those are the two most important items; and if she had to narrow it down to just one, it would be something for the eyes. I'm the same way: If I used a purse that had little slots to hold pens, one of those spaces would be holding my kohl pencil!

Fortunately, we don't have to narrow things down that much. We both have travel kits, which we find indispensable because we're always on the go. And when we find a product that we like, we usually buy two of them: one for home and one to take on the road. If you're on a budget or don't want to carry a full bag with you, narrow it down to the following must-haves, listed in descending order of indispensability:

- **Eye pencils** (for brows and eyeliners): Use the soft kind for anything around the eyes, and a hard pencil for the brows. Even just a little gives a look that's a little more "ancient Egypt." I prefer dark brown or black, but of course your coloring may be different—and don't go with black if you have light hair *and* light skin. You'll look too hard, and you want to remain sensual and alluring.

✻ **Eye shadows:** I use anywhere from two to four different shades (depending on how compact they are)! To create an effortless look with one or two shades, put them on the eyelid. If you're using two colors, you can also put the first under the brow and on the lid, with a darker one in the crease. With three shades, put a medium color on the lid, a darker one in the crease, and the lightest under the brow. Four shades are applied the same as three, except add a fun, even darker color (but not black) under the eye and around the outer corner, lining the top lid—my favorite is royal blue. Believe it or not, my sister and I have actually used even more colors!

✻ **Mascara:** I usually use black because of my coloring. (Sometimes I like using just mascara if I want to open up my eyes in a subtle manner.) I think of this as "bedroom makeup": It doesn't look like you're wearing any color at all, but your eyes look soft. This is a must for any basic kit. (My aunt told me that mascara is also great for quick little gray-hair touch-ups—if you're brunette!)

✻ **Foundation:** This is important for obvious reasons. Get the kind with an SPF so that it doubles as makeup for going out in the sun.

✻ **Powder blush:** Pick a color that will match your lips and nails, if possible. Blush can add pizzazz to your eyes (put it on the crease) and breasts (for a "cleavage" look), and a little on your forehead can bring some warmth on the face. Make sure you also have a brush to apply it.

✻ **Lipstick:** It's important to always make your luscious lips stand out. Keep two shades: lighter lip stains (bedroom

Colors that Flatter

Let your skin tone, hair color, and outfit—along with the occasion—help you choose the best colors for your eyes and lips. Here are some general guidelines, but remember that this is all they are, so don't take them as hard-and-fast rules. Experiment, improvise, and see what happens (and know that as a general rule, blush and lip colors should complement each other).

Flattering Eye Colors

✻ **Blondes:** Lilac, violet, bright yellow (if you have warm skin tones); and orange with peach or gold undertones (especially if you're a golden blonde)

✻ **Brunettes:** Emerald and turquoise

✻ **Redheads:** Earthy green tones, cool blues, and aqua

123

Asian skin: Colors with blue undertones, peach, and dark mustard

Olive skin: Blue with a light or deep, rich tone; and dark yellow or gold with brown undertones

Dark skin: Teal, emerald, hunter green, intense berry, and magenta

Flattering Lip Shades

Light blondes: Wines, berry shades, mauves, brownish "cappuccino" colors, transparent red gloss, pale pinks with blue undertones, and coral (especially in the summer)

Golden blondes: Apricot, peach, coral, and reddish pinks

Blondes with olive skin: Red, warm peaches, browns, and terra-cotta

Brunettes: Almost any shade, including terra-cotta, cinnamon; almost any red; slightly tinted glosses; plums; and almost any pinks (except pastels)

Redheads: Warm terra-cotta, spicy cinnamon red, and peachy browns

Asians and women with yellow skin tones: Bluish reds

Olive skin: Various light and medium wine and burgundy shades; deeper red

Dark skin: Light pinks and rich, dark shades, particularly wines and burgundies

Women with gray or white hair: Intense and darker shades, including plums and wine

124

make-up), because they look so natural, and bold color, such as sizzling-hot red. I like both my lips and eyes to draw attention.

Putting on Your Everyday Face

This is a great way to learn the best way to use basic cosmetics, and then develop your own techniques to achieve the look you want. It's really easy to bring out the facial features you want to play up, minimize the ones you'd rather not call attention to, and tailor your makeup to the occasion. Foundation and blush are designed to help you get your glow on, while eye makeup and lipstick are necessary tools for playing up your most expressive features. In this section, you'll see how to use all of these for your basic daytime look.

Here's the first rule that Veena and I follow: Apply makeup in good light so you can see what you're doing—you might even want to invest in a mirror that has a magnifying side and special lightbulbs. Our years of experience onstage, and in film and television, has given us a great understanding of every aspect of performing and creativity, including the artistry of makeup. Over time, we became very aware that the image you see in the dressing room isn't what appears on camera—or anyplace else. So when applying makeup, consider what kind of light you'll be in (sunlight is the brightest and least "forgiving"). Make sure that you work carefully and with a lighter hand. Every little thing will show up, and thick or poorly blended products will be obvious outdoors—or even if you're inside and facing a bright window.

Finding the right light and thinking about your daily environment is just the beginning. . . .

— **Foundation:** Most of us don't have perfect skin, and the main purpose of foundation is to cover minor imperfections and to even out skin tone. Get a color that blends and matches exactly with your complexion; make sure it's formulated specifically for your skin type (dry, oily, or normal) and has a built-in sunscreen or moisturizer.

Veena and I have found that we like to blend two colors on a palette. We prefer water-based makeup for our normal-to-dry skin, because mineral-oil-based foundation makes both of us break out. For daytime, you may like something that gives you subtle, sheer, or slightly tinted coverage for a natural and even tone. Apply foundation evenly with a sponge.

— **Blush:** Whether you use a cream, gel, or powder form, blush gives your cheeks a rosy, healthy glow. This color should complement or match your lipstick. I like to smile first and start the blush at the "apples" of my cheeks, working my way toward the ears; to contour and create more prominent cheekbones, just brush a

Behind the Smile

This isn't often considered, but do you have a beautiful, attractive smile? Does it show clean, bright teeth and smell sweet? All the lipsticks in the world has minimal impact if you don't take care of your teeth by brushing, flossing, and getting regular dental checkups. If you smoke, be extra mindful of yellow teeth and cigarette breath, which is really unattractive. Even better, stop smoking. Quitting also helps minimize those unwanted vertical lip lines—and the rest of your face will be spared from undesirable wrinkles as well.

darker shade under cheekbone area. I've even used a little dab above the eyelid to give the area a warm look.

— **Powder:** As a finishing touch, set your foundation and blush by pressing powder over your face with a large puff; then dust off the excess with a full brush. This helps your makeup last longer. Translucent powder comes loose in a jar or pressed in a compact.

— **Eyebrow shaping:** In the Middle Eastern and Indian cultures, eyebrows are given special attention because they frame the eyes. Whether lush and earthy or elegantly tapered, these lines give your face expression and play a large role in making you look like *you*. Many people don't think about their eyebrows that much—even professional makeup artists we've worked with don't pay enough attention!

Always use your natural shape as a guide, rather than torturing yourself to achieve a "now" look. We recommend that you have your brows shaped professionally to fit your face. Try more than one method to see which you like best: waxing, plucking, or threading. Then learn how to maintain the shape on your own if you can.

One way isn't better than the other—it's an individual preference. Even my sister and I have different tastes: Veena likes all three choices, but threading is the only method I ever use for hair removal, including having my eyebrows professionally done. I go to an Indian salon for these services; and yes, they do use a regular spool of thread to remove hair!

— **Eyebrow coloring:** Once you've removed the unwanted eyebrow hairs, use a pencil or powder to fill in any gaps or sparse areas. Choose a color to match your hair, or slightly darker if you're blonde. Use light, quick, short strokes to create the shape you want.

Use hard pencils with sharp points for drawing thin "hairs" on the brows; softer pencils can also be used as eyeliners. Pencil can look a little harsh, however, so you might want the gentler effect of a powder, which tends to result in a more natural appearance. I like to "set" the brows with a dark brown powder and a tiny brush.

Alternatively, a tinted or clear brow gel—or even a very light coating of mascara—may be the product for you. To thicken brows naturally, an ancient secret is to apply a little pure castor oil to them nightly; and if they're very light, consider having them dyed professionally.

— **Eyeliner and eye shadow:** Choose colors to complement your eye color and outfits, and always have a neutral shade on hand as a base. To enhance and deepen your eyes, liners are available in pencil, crayon, liquid, powder, or gel form; dark brown works with most eyes. Veena and I like black or even navy blue.

While Middle Eastern and Indian women use the dramatic kohl or surma for day as well as night, most Westerners may want something a little more subtle. For daily wear, try a medium tone in the crease and on the outer half of your lower eyelid; blend well.

— **Eyelashes:** Black mascara is best for brunettes; those with lighter hair should choose dark brown. Get waterproof if you swim, sweat when you're physically active, or have watery eyes; choose a product with lash-builders for enhancement. If you have straight or skimpy lashes—or both—use an eyelash curler to make eyes appear larger, more open, and sexier. Then add mascara; two to three light applications work better than one heavy coat. If they're clumping together, use an eyelash comb to separate them for a more natural look. Some of the makeup artists we work with for print and television work prefer that we wear medium-length false eyelashes (individual or half sets of lashes for the natural look), while others recommend mascara only.

— **Lip color:** To enhance lips, choose colors that complement your coloring and clothing. Moisturizing formulas and those with sunscreen are protective. Veena and I usually prefer products that are vegetable based and made of natural ingredients—they feel so nice!

Although belly dancers tend to emphasize the eyes, my sister and I don't ignore our lips, since we use our whole faces to express emotion when we perform. Wearing just the right shade of lipstick makes my smile show up and helps me get across the meaning of the dance.

To apply lip color, do a little prep work first: Gently rub a damp washcloth over your lips to remove any roughness, and then apply a base. Choose a lip balm (no petroleum jelly—too slick) if you want something to moisturize, and foundation if you want your lipstick to stay on longer (but this can dry your lips, so you'll need to use a moisturizing lipstick over it).

Next, apply lip liner (if you use it). The rule is that you shouldn't line with a darker shade than your lipstick. Starting at the center of your upper lip, draw a line to each outer corner, following the edge of your natural lip line; repeat with the lower lip. Then apply lipstick in one smooth coat. To finish, give yourself a little kiss on the back of your hand; this works better than blotting with a tissue, which removes too much sheen.

To avoid having lipstick show up on your teeth, pucker your mouth into an "O" and insert your index finger between your lips. Slowly pull out your finger, taking excess product with it. Finally, press your lips together to even and set the color.

Hair Makeover

Probably nothing affects your image more dramatically than your hair. That's why having a bad-hair day can be such a drag, and why changing the color or style can bring out parts of your personality that you only suspected were there. Sultry, fiery, cool, sexy, sophisticated, playful, flirty, and youthful—hair expresses them all. We'll help you choose and keep the style and color that are right for your face shape, body, hair type, pocketbook, and personality.

The best everyday hairstyle for you is usually one that works well with your hair's characteristics, your face shape, and your body type. Think about what you want, and then decide if you have the time and money to keep it up—you may need to modify your plans. It will take much less effort and cash if you choose a style that your hair adapts to naturally. Straightening and perming *can* overcome the hair you were born with, but these chemical processes can also damage and change the texture. And, of course, they need to be touched up and redone regularly.

For example, your face shape and body type may be begging you to have long, straight, swinging locks. But if your hair is extremely curly or hangs there like a limp rag, then this style is not for you! You need to find a compromise, or your life will revolve around your struggles with your hair. And don't be a slave to fashion: If everyone is going short this year but that makes you look like a pinhead, don't do it! Keep those tresses a flattering length that's right for *you!*

Once you've found your most flattering cut and color, your stylist can usually update your look with subtle changes. On the other hand, if you're in the mood, don't be too timid to experiment with style or color. The wonderful thing about hair is that it will always grow out, and it can also be covered up!

Traditional Middle Eastern head coverings make a chic and standout impression, especially the wrapped style worn by American Tribal dancers. Veena and I sometimes set off our hair with one of our belly-dance veils worn as a band. And of course, traditional folk dancers in Kashmir, Iran, Afghanistan, and India wear veils on their heads, making head coverings look very feminine.

Offstage, my sister and I love to wear hats. They can really make an outfit, not to mention keep your bad-hair day a secret! And for those special occasions, you can have a lot of fun working with hair color, cut, and style.

Working with Your Hair Type

— **Fine hair** can be very appealing because of its softness, but is often exasperating to style. Go with subtle layers, perhaps add a soft body wave for fullness, and color to enhance the texture.

— **Coarse hair** is usually also thick. This combination can look heavy and needs a great cut to get it under control. Coloring or conditioning can help soften the texture and appearance.

— **Straight hair** that's healthy and shiny can look like a fluid, shimmering curtain. A blunt cut of any length enhances this effect. It's easy to get tired of straight hair, though, and a body wave or setting it in rollers helps give it movement and curves.

— **Curly hair** is best left doing its own marvelous thing. The curves are very appealing, seductive, and flattering to the face. Once in a while for a different look, you might want to try a chemical straightener or blow-dry it straight and use a flatiron for a different look.

Working with Your Face Shape

Next, consider your face shape. Pull your hair back into a ponytail, or if it's short, use a headband to get a clear picture of the outline and structure. Look straight into a mirror. What's the relationship of the width of your forehead to that of your chin—is one much wider than the other? Are your cheekbones the widest part of your face? Look at all of your features and determine your face shape: round, square, long, or heart-shaped. Is your face shaped like an oval? Lucky you! You've hit the jackpot, as this is considered to be the ideal shape for any style, and the right hairdo will bring your face as close as possible to this form.

— If your face shape is **round** with full cheeks and a round chin and hairline, you'll want to take some width away from the sides. Going for a little height on top and keeping the sides sleek and close to your head will elongate and slim the shape. A feathery, wispy effect, where short hair is brought forward onto the face, is also slimming.

— If your face shape is **square** with a wide jaw and forehead, you'll want to have layers and a side part to round the corners. Soft, longish bangs will also help the shape, as will keeping some length at the nape of your neck.

— If you have a **long** face with a narrow jaw- and hairline, you'll want to add width. Layering will create fullness on the sides, and bangs will also shorten the proportions. Avoid long hair reaching below the shoulders, which will pull the focus down.

— If you have a **heart-shaped** face with wide temples and a narrow or pointed chin, add width to the jawline with hair styled in soft layers, in a length that frames your face. Bangs and a side part help narrow the temples.

WORKING WITH YOUR BODY TYPE

— If your body type is **slim,** add a touch of curvaciousness to your appearance with a hairstyle that's curly or wavy with plenty of body and bounce. You can also wear long bangs, layers, and angled cuts to great effect.

— If your body type is **curvy,** complement your form with bangs, a side part, layers, angles, and a medium-length cut.

— If you want **to appear taller,** add a little height to the top but avoid really big hair, which shrinks the rest of you.

HAIR COLOR

Veena and I added red highlights to our dark hair recently, so every once in a while, we find ourselves sitting in salon chairs with little pieces of aluminum foil all over our heads. Our aunt goes the natural route: She colors her hair with henna, which is quite common in both Indian men and women. Veena tried henna at a salon in Bombay when we were in our early 20s.

Our mom used to say, "Henna is good for the hair roots." And it's also good for coloring hair. If you want to try this product, shop wisely, because many products labeled henna aren't pure and may be mixed with other ingredients. Some of these additives are natural plant dyes, but some are metallic salts, including nickel and lead. The only *real* henna stains your hair a translucent red that combines with your natural hair color.

Of course, you may not need to color your hair at all. To bring out your natural shine, try adding a couple of tablespoons of apple-cider vinegar to your final rinse water after shampooing. This removes residues from shampoos and conditioners that can leave hair dull and limp.

To gently lighten and highlight hair, add a couple of tablespoons of lemon juice to your rinse water and then sit in the sun. This works well especially for blondes, as well as brunettes and redheads, and results in a subtle sun-drenched glow. Veena and I did this when we were teenagers, and it brought out the red in our hair.

If you color your hair at home, you may want to find a natural, ammonia-free hair dye that's less harsh on your hair. Whichever product you use, be sure to follow instructions carefully and do a skin test beforehand, as directed on the package. It's possible to damage your hair if you dye or bleach too much or incorrectly, so you might want to consult a professional if hair coloring is new to you, or if you want a change from your current product or shade. It's also very difficult to do highlighting correctly at home. If you make a drastic change in your hair color, don't forget your eyebrows! You may need to have them dyed professionally to match in order to avoid a jarring effect.

Hands and Feet Makeover

When my sister and I belly dance, we bare our feet and use our hands expressively, so keeping them looking pretty is a must. It's no

The Scoop on Henna

Henna is a natural, plant-based dye used to color hair as well as to make beautifully ornate temporary patterns on hands, feet, and other parts of the body. Henna patterns were traditionally used in the Middle East, North Africa, and India to beautify women's hands for celebrations, luck, and the sheer pleasure of the artistry. In very early times, it was a part of religious rituals and is thought to have signified fertility. Wives, concubines, and goddesses all had henna as part of their beauty kits. It was also used to stain fingernails— the first nail polish! Henna body decorations are also known as mehendi, and they're an inexpensive, painless, and temporary alternative to permanent tattoos.

different for everyone else: Your hands are always on display, and your feet come out of hiding in the summer, on vacations in warm climates, and during those intimate moments. Ragged, dirty, unkempt nails (or nails of different lengths) are just plain turnoffs. On the other hand, manicured hands and pedicured feet complete your look and send a message that you care enough to take care of yourself from head to toe.

Whether you do your own mani and pedi or have them done professionally doesn't matter. What's important is that you look well groomed and cared for, and that you choose the right look for you and the occasion.

For all-around versatility, neatness, and elegance, you can't beat the natural look of softly buffed nails or a chic and clean French manicure. Every color you wear is an extension of your mood. For example, red nail polish is a classic color and a favorite among women in the Middle East and India. My cousin in India says it makes her feel "hot"!

I like to experiment with different colors. One week it might be a bright, sunny orange, the next week I'll prefer a pearly silver color. We both like the variety in our nail polish because we wear different costumes all the time, and I like to match—even greens and purples! These wild colors aren't just fun, they complete the statements that our costumes make. The same rule applies to clothing for other occasions: The best look is for polish to match or at least harmonize with your clothes, and it's better if your fingernails match your toes. Even if no one sees your feet, *you'll* know.

For every day, muted or neutral colors are best, but they don't have to look boring. I have so many neutrals with tints of peach, pink, or frosty tones . . . and they complement almost everything.

Watch out for chipped polish, which looks careless and sloppy. In both the Middle East and India, hands are considered very sensual. So if you use your hands a lot and are too busy to maintain a deeper color that makes chipping highly visible, a neutral shade or a French manicure may be best for you.

It doesn't matter if you have long or short nails. But, if you have short nails and would like a change, consider getting acrylics for special occasions—or just for fun! Imagine lightly and playfully scratching your lover with those sensual claws . . . meow!

Beautify Yourself for a Night Out on the Town

Okay, girls, let's go crazy! After dark is the right time for glitter and glam that does your out-on-the-town outfit justice. And now that you've gotten savvy and skilled with basic makeup and other beauty techniques, you're ready to be more inventive . . . maybe even a little wild.

Nighttime is when you can really let loose and use colors, products, ideas, and techniques that might be inappropriate for the day. Set aside some time before your next big night out to experiment with your new toys. Don't be shy—remember that all cosmetics are temporary, and they'll wash off so that you can start over. It's always more fun to do this with friends, and the more the merrier! To practice, you might want to have some pals over for a makeup party. This can be lots of fun and gets everybody's creative juices flowing. For some quick inspiration, take a look at some of our favorite nighttime beautifying moves:

FACE

— **Concealer:** Begin your transformation with concealer, which acts like a wonderful eraser of flaws. This liquid or stick needs to be two shades lighter than your base foundation. Use it to cover up dark circles under your eyes (which many women have naturally and which can worsen with too little sleep), to hide blemishes, and sometimes to reduce redness around the nose or cheeks. I sometimes use it to cover a couple of extra moles.

You may also use a little concealer between your inner eye and your nose; discoloration in this area is often overlooked but can make you look pinched and tired. Some women also have a darkness at the outer edge, where the upper and lower eyelids join; this makes your eyes look pulled down, but disappears when you use concealer. Veena and I also use it for highlighting cheekbones and the jawline area (as explained in "Contouring" below).

— **Foundation:** For nighttime foundation, my sister and I like to wear a slightly thicker or creamier formula all over our faces; again, water-based is best for me. Make sure that you blend it along the jaw—you want to avoid that telltale line!

— **Contouring:** This technique can subtly change the shape and prominence of your facial features, using two shades of foundation. One is a shade lighter and the other is a shade darker than your base foundation; there are also contouring powders you apply with a brush. The paler color catches the light and brings a surface forward; the deeper one causes the area to recede or look smaller.

If you want to do this, be sure to practice *a lot* and blend *very* well before going out in public. Use a light touch and go for subtle shading and highlighting. It's actually quite simple to do once you have the knack—but if the effect is obvious, then what's the point? That's not the kind of attention you want!

Here are ways to handle the most common contouring areas. Use these same principles to minimize a double chin or any other facial feature you'd like to be less noticeable.

- ▓ **To make a wide nose look narrower:** Apply the darker shade of foundation along the sides of your nose, starting at the level of your inner-eye corner and ending at the tip of each side of the nose. Then apply a narrow band of lighter foundation down the middle of the nose, starting at the center point and stopping just before the tip.

- ▓ **To make a long nose look shorter:** Apply a dot of darker foundation on the very tip and just under the tip of your nose.

- ▓ **To slenderize a wide or heavy jaw:** Make a row of dots using the darker foundation along the jawline and chin.

- ▓ **To bring out your cheekbones:** Apply a lighter foundation just above the cheekbones, and a darker foundation below them.

- ▓ **To widen a narrow jaw and soften a pointed chin:** Make a row of dots using the lighter foundation along your jaw and chin.

— **Blush:** You might want to go a shade more intense for nighttime. Some of the deeper shades may also be used for contouring, in addition to (or instead of) the darker foundation.

— **Powder:** Dust your face lightly with a translucent loose powder after the blush for a matte look. This is where you don't need to look shiny. (We'll let the finishing glitter take care of that!) Or you might want to dust pearlized powder over your forehead and cheeks for an extra special glow.

Note: If you have wrinkles around your eyes, you may want to omit concealer and powder because they'll make the lines look more prominent.

EYES

— **Color:** A quick, easy way to give your daytime look more glamour is to simply use more of everything. For example, you can intensify with heavier eye shadow and eyeliner and an extra coat or two of thickening mascara. Or go with a darker brown or black for the smoky, kohl-inspired look. But for a truly special occasion, change the colors, too—everything can be a little brighter for night-time. Choose your eye shadow to match your clothes: iridescent versions of their colors or metallics, such as gold, silver, copper, and bronze.

We still love surma or kohl, and when we go to Egypt or India, we always bring some of the modern version with us. You can duplicate this look with dark brown, gray, or black eye shadow and eyeliner: Apply neutral shadow over the entire lid area, and then put a darker one in the crease under the brow bone. Apply the same neutral color to your lower-lash rim and smudge it with a cotton swab. Finish by drawing a line on your top lid with the eyeliner; keep it close to the lashes and extend it slightly beyond the corner of your eye. This is a dramatic, smoky, sultry look that says "Wow!"

— **Lashes:** Fake lashes can give you an extra touch of glamour for a night on the town. If you have unusually skimpy lashes, you even might want to use these boosters for daytime wear. Just make sure that they aren't too thick or dark, and that you trim them so that they're neither too wide for your eye nor so long that you have that "surprised doll" look. The individual kind is very natural looking. Dark brown is the best color for false eyelashes unless you're a woman of color—then black is fine.

Veena and I sometimes wear artificial lashes when performing or for television or photo shoots. I prefer "half" lashes, which are full lashes cut in two. They're natural and easier to wear.

— **Bindis:** Nothing attracts attention more than wearing a small beautiful dot in the middle of your forehead! When we were kids, our mother had many different kinds of these, called *bindis,* and we used to play and experiment wearing them. They're self-adhesive, so they didn't make a mess (today they come in different shapes and styles, even jeweled).

We'd stick these little dots on different areas of our faces, body, and bellies. We'd put them around the eyes, the outside and inside cor-

Bindis

As mentioned earlier, bindis are the small dots traditionally made by applying a red powder to a woman's or man's forehead. The word is derived from the Sanskrit for "dot" or "drop." They're usually placed between the eyebrows signifying the mystic third eye or sixth chakra. Today there are a zillion self-stick designs in bright colors to wear as a fashion statement, and there are even large ones to wear around the belly button.

135

ners—and it turns out that this is a popular way to wear them now! Don't worry, you don't have to be Indian to wear these alluring marks on your forehead. Many women use them to feel more centered, confident, and exotic . . . and they draw attention to your gorgeous eyes.

LIPS

For nighttime pizzazz, make your lipstick brighter and your lips fuller. For a pouty, sexy mouth, emphasize your top lip by dabbing just a touch of gloss in the center; you can also apply a dab of a light-colored shimmering eye shadow (such as pink, gold, or white) on the middle of your lower lip on top of your lipstick to make them look even fuller. Veena and I often use this technique when we perform.

- **To make the most of thin lips:** Create the illusion of fuller lips with makeup. Big, sensual lips go in and out of fashion, but a luscious mouth always looks sexy. First, choose light or medium shades of lipstick because darker ones make lips look thinner (the same principle as dark clothing making you look slimmer). Start with a lip pencil in a neutral color and outline, drawing slightly beyond your lip line—and we do mean *slightly,* since nothing looks more ridiculous than going way over the line. Then apply lipstick, using that outline as your guide. If you want fuller lips but prefer the natural look, use the same technique with a pencil the same shade as your lips and a natural-colored gloss, blending in the edges of the pencil.

- **To minimize full lips:** You can also fool the eye with makeup to achieve this goal. We like the look of bigger lips, so we consider women who have them to be blessed. On the other hand, an overly prominent pucker can distract too much from the eyes. So to begin to minimize, line just inside the lips with a pencil that's one shade darker than your natural color. Fill in with matte lipstick rather than glossier types, and stick with darker colors, which make your lips look smaller. Muted colors such as plums and brownish tones also work well for this.

- **To keep lips kissable:** Go easy on the lipstick, since men generally like the way it looks, but not the way it feels or tastes. Instead of glossy color, try matte finishes that are less gooey. Lip stains, which leave maximum color with minimum residue, are another alternative. In ancient times, stains were made from natural dyes in berries and other plants, and heightened color to make lips more alluring. These days, you can find lipstains, which look natural and are a good choice for workouts . . . and other situations that call for a natural look, if you know what I mean!

HAIR

Typically, belly dancers have long hair that they wear loose and flowing so that it moves beguilingly along with their bodies. This is a sensual look for nighttime. If you prefer a short style but want to play with the idea of long hair, try some extensions, weaves, or other hairpieces. We've often seen how longer locks—including fake ones—can bring out the sensuality and playfulness in a woman. Even just pulling your hair back and clipping on a faux ponytail can change the type of energy you feel and project.

And why stop there? There are so many other ways to change your hair's appearance: straightening, curling, crimping, gels, and mousses . . . and sprays in clear, wild, or subtle colors, and glitters. . . . The possibilities for creativity are endless, no matter what the length or texture of your tresses. Veena and I love to wear hair jewelry, clips, and headbands, too, which are especially cool when they match the fabric in our outfits.

137

BELLY AND BODY

— **Makeup:** If we're baring our midriffs, my sister and I enhance our bellies, too—we'll smooth on a shimmery body cream for a really nice effect. If you have bare shoulders or a plunging neckline, shimmer lotions will nicely draw the eyes to those areas, or just dust a little translucent pearlescent powder over the exposed skin. Applying a foundation or body makeup to your belly helps even out the color and cover scars and stretch marks or other trouble spots. You can even use the contouring technique explained earlier (page 132) to give the illusion of a somewhat smaller, tauter, more muscled belly—why not try it just for fun? You can also brush a little contouring between your breasts for "cleavage."

— **Decorations:** There's so much belly decoration to choose from right now, from bindis to real and fake pierced jewelry to tattoos. My sister and I sometimes wear big jeweled bindis over our belly buttons. Body art is in, and we love to wear intricate henna tattoos on our hands, feet, and bellies. Neither of us has permanent tattoos because we like to change our designs, which the temporary henna allows us to do. (But if I did have actual ink, it would be in a place where only that special someone could see it!)

Curtains Up!

Cosmetics can help you look your best, and looking good enhances your self-esteem and confidence. This will make you a better dancer, lover, student, professional, mother, or daughter. Now that you've put the icing on the cake, (naturally sweetened, of course!), you're ready to present your yummy self to the world and project what's inside. Go on—reap the rewards of all your efforts . . . of knowing your unique qualities and how to play them up . . . of opening up your mind to new possibilities and to your inner voice and intuition . . . of eating well and pleasurably . . . and of dancing your way to shapelier body.

You've got the costumes for every occasion and know how to use cosmetics to complete the picture. The spotlight's on you—you're the star performer of your own life. So, are you ready for your close-up?

※※※　※※※

Chapter Eight

LOVE YOUR BELLY . . . STRUT YOUR STUFF

BY VEENA

Now *you're* ready to show off on a bigger stage—the stage of life! Remember, you're the star of your own journey—the main performer. Your ovations are the way that those you know show their appreciation and love. You're making changes for yourself, but also for other people . . . to get their attention, feedback, and applause.

You've done a lot of preparation for you "opening night." Your pride in your accomplishments, increased confidence, and self-esteem give you that extra something that draws more people to you. And because you've increased your sensuality, the joy you experience in the way your own body feels and moves and in the way the world impacts all your awakened senses will create even more magnetism. The new you is going to get a bigger, more adoring audience, starting with close friends, then co-workers, and finally out in the "real world." It doesn't matter if your audience is one or one million—they're all special to you, as you are to them.

Having made an effort and succeeded over the course of this book gives you added confidence and self-esteem. You can actually feel and see the difference! And a bonus is that you've done it using the health-building route of good eating, regular exercise, doing things you enjoy, and surrounding yourself with beautiful colors and gorgeous textures, rather than through unhealthy crash dieting, pills, deprivation, and punishment.

Looking good will make you feel good, and feeling good will give you a standing ovation in everything you do as a career woman, a mom, a friend, and a lover. Everyone has an audience, and yours is what's important to you. If you want to hear more than you've been getting, the principles in this book can take you there.

Setting the Scene

There are a variety of techniques that create a specific tone and atmosphere on an empty stage. When my sister and I are dancing, we often use different sets and various props to set the mood and the look to accompany us. The same is true when you plan a fun evening at home. So whether you're your own audience or have that special someone or friends in mind, let's really get it going with a few simple, easy props. . . .

142

▓ **Clean slate:** Make sure your space is clear of clutter so that you have room to dance.

▓ **Set dressing:** Some exotic Indian silk saris can elegantly drape the walls and also cover some throw pillows to put on the floor and/or on the bed.

▓ **Lighting:** Use lamps, candles, and/or soft ceiling lights, not fluorescents.

This is how Neena and I live our lives: We wear costumes that fit; that is, we don't show up ill-prepared in sloppy, torn-up clothes. So don't show up for your life in your old sweats! If you do, how can we see the real you? Show respect and love not only for yourself, but also for your audience—put your best foot forward and give them a reason to respect and love you back.

When Neena and I prepare for our shows, we pick, arrange, and get to know the music; create and rehearse the choreography; design our costumes, jewelry, hair, and makeup; and voilà—it's showtime! It's a lot of work, but we do it because we know it shows in our performance, and because we care about our audience. We enjoy our work, it's our labor of love. And while my sister and I do love the process of preparing and doing the work, we love the result even more. The feedback is worth the effort. When we perform, I feel waves of love and appreciation from our audience because of the effort we put into our performance, and because we did a good job. That's our reward.

Live Life to the Max

Following our philosophy will increase your sensuality and boost your awareness of the world around you. Now get out there and live your life, using all your heightened senses—including your sixth sense—to tune in to what you desire to do. Do what you love: Take belly-dance, art, or voice lessons; go to the foreign-film festival alone or with friends; join a hiking group; volunteer to teach someone to read. Everything you do, do it the belly way—with passion, love, and attention to detail. When you follow this path, love will come to you in exotic and mysterious ways.

So whether it's through an audience of millions on national television or a live audience of that one special guy in your life, or your group of girlfriends, everyone you meet is unique—each is different and wonderful. No matter where you are, you're a performer with an audience . . . and you don't have to belly dance to get there!

BE DARING

It's natural to get a little stage fright—even the best performers still do, including Neena and me. Fear artificially protects you from harm, and it shouldn't stop you from getting out the backstage door and on with your life. How can people love you if they don't see you? Expand your horizons gradually if you need to, and use your belly intuition. Know where your comfort level is and look before you leap—or maybe take a small step instead. Skydiving may be too big a change for you right now, but you *can* sign up for a belly-dance class and get that temporary henna tattoo!

Take things at *your* speed, not what others are pushing for. If you're going too fast, you won't enjoy the process or results, but going too slow is like keeping your audience waiting—with the curtain already up! Being too timid means that what you want might not be around anymore when you're finally ready—from someone you want to attract, to a job, a friend, or an apartment . . . or even a gorgeous, one-of-a-kind, marked-down dress.

So now that you've expanded your risk-taking comfort level, take a *big* chance. Nobody pays attention to the belly dancer onstage who makes itty-bitty movements or takes tiny steps while dressed in drab gray sweats. Make a big bold gesture or you'll lose your audience. Be bold in your inner and outer self so that you'll be able to recognize and grab opportunities in love and career. Now that you're more secure, confident, and looking good, go out and sing at the top of your lungs on whatever "stage" your life provides. Even if you're shy, make a bold statement every now and then so that people can notice you and see just how fabulous you are. Flash a really big smile at the next cute guy that catches your eye—just make sure you're looking good and wearing a flattering shade of lipstick!

Fragrance: Aromatherapy oils, potpourri, incense, and scented candles give a sexy, sensual scent.

Food: Cook a romantic, homemade, healthy Middle Eastern (or Indian) dinner, appetizer, or dessert. If you've already had dinner, plan for a suggested appetizer, snack, or dessert from our Belly Café Menu (page 151).

Props: If your audience is your significant other, set out some fun toys for the two of you to play with, such as massage oils and the like.

Music: Turn on some belly-dance music, of course! If you want something slow and sensual, play one of the taksims. It will certainly set the mood for anything. . . .

143

Lights, Video Camera, Action!

Okay, so you've seen the "before" in earlier chapters; now let's take a look at the "after." You've practiced your sexy workout, applied a new style of makeup, gotten a different wardrobe, relaxed with spa techniques, and tasted yummy new foods. Now, the moment of truth has arrived: Videotape yourself again. Do the same thing you did the first time: Walk, stop, make a 180-degree turn, and walk the other way. Then take a belly breath, face the camera, and describe yourself again.

Now, play back both videos (first the "before" and then "after") and see the results of your efforts. How do you like this new transformation? After you've decided what *you* think, ask your significant other. Does he like what he sees? What about others, such as family and friends? They don't have to know the specifics of *what* changes occurred—it'll be your secret. All they need to know is that they're seeing the real, ultimate, and unique *you*.

Just remember, you can videotape yourself more than once in order to monitor yourself, your dance progress, or the new changes on your body. You can even have your friends record you—that way you can tape in front of a live audience!

Spotlight Your Talents and Strengths . . . and Accept Yourself

At some point, trying to "fix" your flaws takes time away from developing your strengths. Your strong points are the places where you can buff, polish, adorn yourself . . . and really shine. Now that you've made over your physical aspects, concentrate on building your talents and then doing good things with them. If you love to sing, give a performance with some friends at a karaoke bar. If you're a great cook, design a meal with passion and perform for your audience: family friends, or more—you decide! If you have a love for sports, take tennis (or whatever) lessons. And dance away from doing hurtful, destructive things to yourself and others.

Also, keep in mind that nonstop perfect is imperfect. After all, what makes your heart strings go "plink-a-plink" about a puppy? It's the way one of his ears flops to one side and he's got that goofy eagerness to crawl all over you. We usually find this lopsidedness endearing in people, too: Maybe you smile at someone's overbite, go limp at his crooked smile, sigh over a raspy voice, or find it hilarious when someone sings off-key at a karaoke bar. Well, these kinds of flaws make *you* lovable, too.

Like many people, in my early teens, I used to see each of my flaws as something that made me feel inferior. But what I didn't like in myself was considered a jewel by the first guy I had a crush on. So accept yourself and embrace the clumsy, geeky, silly, and charming things in yourself and others. After all, some of the goofiest people make terrific dance partners! Physical quirks aren't flaws; they're character signatures that makes each of us unique and special.

Pass It On

Love is one of those things that continues to expand and grow: There's never a limit to how many people you can love and how deeply you can care for them. The more you have for yourself, the more you can give to others . . . and others have more for you. Basically, the greater the love you have, the more you attract. It just keeps expanding and getting passed on to others. I believe that this is the best and most effective way of getting and keeping your "audience." You don't even have to advertise for people to show up to your gig—they'll just come! And maybe *they'll* be inspired by you.

But you have to *want* to change, and love yourself enough to transform your life. Even if it's just trying a new shade of lipstick, it counts! Neena and I have inspired so many women to spice up their wardrobes, their makeup, their workouts, and their love lives that we know you can do it, too. We've also showed people how to follow their belly and pursue a dream, in spite of whatever obstacles life might put in their way.

We've received tons of e-mails from people all over the world, including many from our own culture, who said that they loved themselves enough to pursue their own goals, and not those of their spouses, parents, grandparents, and children . . . and that they would never have considered it in the past due to family pressures. One fan wrote: "Thanks for opening the door for me! I am now pursuing a life I love—writing!"

But we feel that *we* didn't open the door for her—the opportunity was already there. And that's what we're saying to you: The door *is* open, and you just have to walk through it! Pretty simple, huh? For us, being true to ourselves allowed us to go through the door to hundreds of passions and to pursue a talent that we'd only dreamed about in that farmhouse living room in front of the old, broken stereo.

101 Belly Ways to Give and Get Love

Here are 101 ideas for giving and getting love in your relationships with yourself, your lover, and your friends and family. (It's not quite 1,001 Arabian nights, but hey, it's a start!) We hope that you'll go beyond the suggestions we've provided: Pay a return visit to each chapter to come up with your own ideas for ways that are uniquely *you* or uniquely *them*. (That's what the blank lines are for. Hint: People usually give you what they'd like to get in return.)

Try to include all five senses, and use your sixth sense to tell you if what you're planning feels right. Be creative, silly, and wild . . . and above all, be loving! Since there's often a fine line between giving and getting love (and no line at all when you're considering yourself), and since giving love often means getting love in return (and vice versa), we've made no distinction in our lists between giving and getting.

GIVING AND GETTING LOVE: YOURSELF

1. Enroll in belly-dance classes.
2. Take a mental-health day off from work.
3. Read books and articles that entertain you or expand your mind—whatever you need at the moment.
4. Give yourself permission to relax for a few minutes in the middle of a busy, stressful day.
5. Prepare a delicious, healthful meal for yourself.
6. Have nutritious snacks ready *before* you get hungry, and you'll love yourself slim.
7. Take a break when you need it, and treat yourself to a richly aromatic cup of Moroccan mint tea.
8. Take a walk in nature.
9. Splurge on an expensive haircut.
10. Have your makeup done professionally.
11. Get a (temporary) henna tattoo—maybe a tribal chain on your upper arm.
12. Take a warm, aromatic bath.
13. Book a massage.
14. Have a manicure.
15. Get a pedicure.
16. Wear beautiful silk nightclothes, even when you're sleeping alone.
17. Sleep on clean, high-quality, pure-cotton sheets.
18. Keep your skin soft with a nice body lotion and a fragrance you love.
19. Buy a fluffy sweater that feels *gooood* on your skin.
20. Listen to music that makes your soul sing.
21. Dance to your heart's content to music that energizes you.
22. Try a new food.
23. Go to a museum or gallery and look at beautiful art.
24. Buy a fragrant bouquet and keep it where you can smell it all day.

25.   Tell yourself when you've done a good job.
26.   Give yourself some alone time when you need it.
27.   Say no and yes when you want to.
28.   Belly dance for yourself.
29.   _____
30.   _____
31.   _____

GIVING AND GETTING LOVE: YOUR LOVER

32.   Ask your lover about his favorite foods, colors, movies, and so forth.
33.   Bring your lover breakfast in bed.
34.   Take him out for a romantic dinner.
35.   Find foods that you both enjoy as sensual pleasures.
36.   Feed him with your fingers.
37.   Wear a sexy negligee.
38.   Choose sexy lingerie.
39.   Go without underwear.
40.   Leave little love notes on the bed pillows, bathroom mirror, or refrigerator door.
41.   Make a gift basket of sensual goodies (scented oils, body lotion, sexy underwear, and the like) and leave it on the bed for your lover to find.
42.   Use a perfume that will enhance his mood.
43.   Use a delicious-smelling conditioner to attract your lover to smell and touch your hair.
44.   Strategically place scented candles in the bedroom.
45.   Give a massage—whole body or just hands, feet, or head/scalp.
46.   Ask what your partner wants in bed.
47.   Tell him what *you* want in bed.
48.   Give your lover a scented-oil rubdown.
49.   Touch your lover often.
50.   Take the phone off the hook for uninterrupted time together.
51.   Join your partner in something *he* likes to do.
52.   Find out what kind of music turns your lover on.

53. Listen to him with your head, heart, *and* belly.
54. Tell your lover why you appreciate him.
55. Play strip poker and other games of seduction, or pretend you're characters in a movie.
56. Whisper sweet nothings in his ear.
57. Gently tell them what you expect of him.
58. Gently tell him when you've had enough.
59. Treat him to a quick romantic getaway—even just for a day or a weekend.
60. Read love poems to each other.
61. Ask for a relaxing hand or foot massage (no tickling!).
62. Surprise him with a henna tattoo.
63. Ask your lover to brush your hair.
64. Ask for a hug.
65. Take a warm, aromatic bath together.
66. Belly dance for him!
67. _____
68. _____
69. _____

GIVING AND GETTING LOVE: YOUR FRIENDS AND FAMILY

70. Find out what your friends' favorite activities are.
71. Offer your friends your time and/or your services, especially when they're in a crunch.
72. Visit your friends when they're sick, and perhaps bring them some hot chicken soup.
73. Be extra kind when they're stressed out.
74. Offer to take care of their pets and plants or take in their mail when they travel.
75. Be generous in your communication: Let them know when they do something that pleases you.
76. Find ways to make them laugh.
77. Watch a good movie so that you can laugh and cry together.
78. Make a delicious Middle Eastern meal for yourself and share it with someone.
79. Take a favorite dessert to your friend's house and share a sweet treat.
80. Have a belly-wear party.
81. Have a girls' belly-dance party and boogie to our DVD.

82. Send friends homemade greeting cards to lighten up their day and let them know you're thinking of them.
83. If you're good with colors, offer to help your friend select the best colors for them.
84. Buy someone flowers for no reason.
85. Buy them a colorful silk or chenille scarf.
86. Compliment your friends on the softness of their coats or sweaters.
87. Reassure them nonverbally with a gentle touch or pat on the shoulder.
88. Call them on their birthday and sing "Happy Birthday" or a favorite song.
89. Treat them to a concert by their favorite performer.
90. Tell them how much you love them.
91. Share a good joke—or better yet, a "bad" one!
92. Compliment them on a job well done.
93. Tell them, "I understand," and mean it.
94. Go on a carousel ride together.
95. Practice good etiquette, such as always saying "Please" and "Thank you."
96. Ask for a hug.
97. Give them a hug.
98. Belly dance for them!
99. _____
100. _____
101. _____

Keep Moving . . . So the Beat Goes On

True love is not a one-night stand! It goes on forever. Life is change and movement in the same way that dance is, with the movements always morphing into something else. The next part might be traveling forward (remember those traveling belly-dance steps?), twirling in circles ("look at all aspects of me"), or just staying in one place—sometimes dance includes a moment of stillness (everyone needs a rest!).

Life and love are circular, like belly-dance movements—as you take things in, you also give out to the world. So love the results of this book, and love yourself enough to keep up the changes you've made . . . and perhaps keep on making new ones. Continue transforming yourself in big and little ways every day. Look for new directions, and never stop learning about and taking care of yourself.

The book is done, but you're not. This is the last chapter of this volume, but it's the first chapter of your new life!

✳✳✳ ✳✳✳

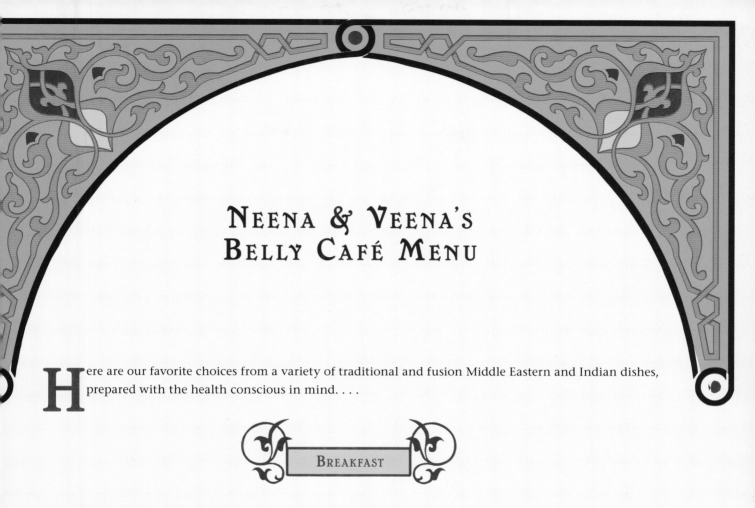

Neena & Veena's Belly Café Menu

Here are our favorite choices from a variety of traditional and fusion Middle Eastern and Indian dishes, prepared with the health conscious in mind. . . .

Breakfast

Dancers' favorite fruit bowl: (In season) organic Granny Smith apples, pineapples, berries, oranges, grapefruits, kiwi, and pomegranates with lemon juice and a sprinkle of paprika.

Melon kabobs: A variety of organic, juicy melons—including honeydew and cantaloupe—cubed and put on a skewer.

Himalayan quinoa: Served with pistachio nuts, shredded coconut, and goji berries; topped with muscovado sugar and your choice of coconut, almond, or rice milk.

Quinoa: Served with pine nuts and lysium berries; topped with maple crystals and your choice of almond, soy, oat, or rice milk.

Steel-cut oatmeal: Serve hot with walnuts and top with a touch of pure maple syrup and vanilla, your choice of almond, oat, soy, or rice milk.

Crispy or puffed rice: Organic brown-rice cereal with sliced organic bananas served with cold almond, rice, oat, or soy milk.

Jordanian healthy omelette: All egg whites, stuffed with fresh sautéed garlic, onions, in-season veggies, ground lamb, and exotic spices; served with a side of sliced tomatoes.

Raw muesli: Organic rolled oats, as well as spelt, barley, kamut, chopped almonds, pecans, and dried lysium berries; served with cold oat or almond milk.

Ful madamis: Fava beans served with a side of hard-boiled eggs, parsley, lemon wedges, and olive oil. An Egyptian favorite for breakfast!

LUNCH

Grilled-salmon Caesar salad: Romaine lettuce, avocados, flaxseed croutons, choice of shredded Parmesan or almond cheese, and "belly vinaigrette" (olive oil, lemon juice, aminos, and spices).

Cal-Asian-fusion veggie wrap: Shiitake mushrooms, avocados, shredded carrots, cucumbers, greens, sprouts, bits of tomatoes, asparagus, and tahini sauce.

Triple-threat vegan special: Veggie soup (vegetables galore!); veggie salad with belly vinaigrette dressing; and half of a veggie sandwich (cucumbers; shredded carrots and zucchini; organic greens; sprouts; sautéed portabella mushroom; avocados; almond, soy, or rice cheese; vegan mayo; Dijon mustard; and tahini sauce on sprouted manna bread).

Healthy Indian veggie pizza: Choice of homemade tomato or pesto sauce with mild Indian spices; low-fat goat, mozzarella, or almond cheese; sliced tomatoes; and bits of cauliflower, peas, potatoes, bell peppers, mushrooms, and red onions on a whole-wheat chapati.

Vegan Indian taali: Okra, saag (spinach and mustard greens), and eggplant cooked in very mild Indian spices; served with whole-wheat gobi paratha (tortilla stuffed with cauliflower).

Mediterranean cabbage rolls: Your choice of organic, vegetarian-fed lamb or beef and mild spices. An Armenian favorite!

Algerian couscous: Lamb or chicken, organic veggies, and spices . . . mmmm!

Egyptian vegan tablich: Organic zucchini, green beans, curry, and other spices served over steamed brown rice.

Peanut butter and jelly: For the kid in all of us (except no peanuts and no jelly)! Organic macadamia-nut butter and raw honey on top of manna bread (or a brown-rice cake).

153

APPETIZERS, SOUPS, AND SALADS

Middle Eastern vegan chips and salsa tray: Spicy brown-rice chips and a variety of vegetable "chips" (dried veggie slices) served with hummus (chickpeas), fava-bean dip, lentil pâté, and baba ghanoush (eggplant).

Samosas: Choice of vegan or nonvegan (lamb or mutton): smashed red potatoes, green peas, and Indian spices wrapped and baked in chickpea or whole-wheat chapati.

Yogi shorba: Red- and yellow-lentil soup with garlic, onions, and mild Indian spices; served with Indian flat bread.

Vegan Israeli butternut-squash soup: Has mild spices; served with sprouted-wheat flat bread.

Tabouli: Fresh parsley, mint, choice of bulgur wheat or wheat-free quinoa, organic cucumbers, red onions, tomatoes, and olive oil. A favorite in Lebanon and Israel!

Salatat: Salad from the Middle Eastern and Gulf region containing eggplant, garlic, lemon juice, and spices.

Healthy Greek salad: Fresh, organic greens and romaine lettuce, fresh goat cheese, cucumbers, Peruvian olives, and dressing.

Greek dolmas: Organic brown rice, pine nuts, currants, fresh herbs, and spices wrapped in grape leaves. A Mediterranean favorite!

Tunisian potato salad: Organic red potatoes, olives, fresh herbs, and mild spices.

Raw-veggie plate: A variety of raw, organic veggies with several dipping sauces and nut butters.

Red Sea seaweed salad: A variety of seaweed, hemp oil, finely minced fresh garlic, fresh mint, and mild spices.

SIDE DISHES

Dairy-free smashed potatoes: Mashed red potatoes and exotic spices.

Steamed organic asparagus: Served with fresh garlic and olive oil.

Healthy Persian rice: Steamed brown rice, fresh dill, lima beans, and saffron.

Sautéed organic greens: Your choice of spinach, kale, or mustard greens with fresh garlic and olive oil.

Healthy Israeli couscous: Served with fresh veggies and spices.

Eastern–style organic grains: Steamed millet, quinoa, and/or brown rice with currants, almonds, and spices.

Organic wild rice: Steamed and served with sea salt.

DINNER

Venison: Cooked to perfection and served on top of sautéed kale.

South Indian fish stew: Scallops, mussels, shrimp, octopus, and mild Goan spices.

Cairo kabobs: Cubed grass-fed lamb loins, green and red peppers, onions, fresh garlic, cherry tomatoes, and whole mushrooms—all put on a skewer.

Vegetarian Indian lentil loaf: Served with your choice of okra, saag, or eggplant cooked in mild Indian spices.

Spicy Pakistani-Asian stir-fry: A variety of fresh, organic veggies (including broccoli, cabbage, cauliflower, red onions, green peas, fresh garlic, and ginger) stir-fried in exotic spices with light extra-virgin coconut or olive oil. Your choice of cage-free, hormone-free chicken-breast strips; organic, corn-fed beef strips; or pure veggies served on top of steamed brown rice.

Healthy Asian-Afghani angel-hair pasta: Mung-bean pasta, fresh garlic, cilantro-pesto sauce, fresh herbs, sun-dried tomatoes, seaweed, shiitake mushrooms, cauliflower, a dash of turmeric and mild spices; topped with shredded almond cheese; served with sprouted manna bread.

Moroccan-style lemon chicken: Hormone-free, cage-free, skinless chicken, North African spices, fresh ginger, saffron, and olives; served with asparagus and yellow beets.

Herb-roasted turkey: Skinless turkey breast, garlic, and herbs; served with Brussels sprouts and red beets. A Thanksgiving favorite!

Kashmiri lotus root: Lotus-root curry, served with Kashmiri palao (rice), rose petals, and spices.

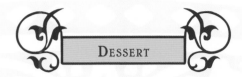

DESSERT

Vegan chocolate torte: Organic cocoa, almonds, dates, agave, and coconut.

Raw-coconut puffs: Sprouted cashews, coconut, birch, and vanilla.

Moroccan chocolate bonbons: Organic chocolate, dried dates, apricots, walnuts, and pine nuts, sweetened with agave.

Vegan cheese-and-crackers tray: Dessert doesn't always have to be super sweet. A variety of nondairy cheeses and brown-rice, sesame-seed crackers, and flaxseed crackers is a great way to relax after a meal, especially when accompanied by a glass of organic wine!

Vegan Middle Eastern rice pudding: Brown rice, almond milk, rosewater, pistachios, and maple syrup; sprinkled with cinnamon. A favorite in India (*kheer*) and the Middle East!

Carob halvah: Sesame seeds, carob, and pure raw honey.

Healthy karah: Amaranth, cardamom, cinnamon, and raw muscovado sugar. A much-healthier version of a favorite Punjabi dish!

Mediterranean fruit bowl: (In season) organic apples, mangos, peaches, nectarines, apricots, pears, bananas, dates, persimmons, figs, grapes, papayas, cherries, and dried fruits.

Root-beer float: Pure, natural root beer, topped with vanilla rice-milk ice cream.

BEVERAGES

Breakfast smoothie: Fresh organic bananas, apples, berries (in season), pear juice, crushed ice, and bee pollen.

Vitamin-C breakfast blast: Fresh-squeezed lemon, orange, and/or grapefruit juice; filtered water; Emer'gen-C; and a twist of orange (or a slice).

Fruit-juice fast: Organic, fresh fruits that are in season.

Veggie-fast blast: Organic celery, spinach, beets, cucumbers, parsley, ginger, lemon, and spirulina.

Middle Eastern lemonade: Organic lemon juice, orange blossom, rosewater, and fresh mint leaves; sweetened with stevia and served with a dash of cayenne (optional). Refreshing!

Eastern pomegranate drink: Fresh pure juice with a touch of orange blossom and rosewater.

Natural soda: Kombucha tea, which is a naturally carbonated drink; your choice of green or black tea. Great for the digestion!

Refreshing mint-yogurt drink: Just like it sounds! This is a favorite in Middle East, North Africa, Pakistan, and India.

Herbal chai: Naturally decaf with Indian spices; served with low-fat goat's, almond, or soy milk. Tastes just like Mom's!

Green Moroccan mint tea: Pure green tea, fresh mint leaves, and raw honey.

Traditional hot cocoa: Organic cocoa sweetened with stevia. Warming for the belly!

Cocoa amandine: Organic cocoa, almond milk (sweetened with cane juice), and vanilla; served hot or cold.

157

Turkish coffee: Caffeine-free! Herbal tea that tastes like coffee.

Wine spritzer: Organic, sulfite-free red or white wine and sparkling water, with a twist.

Nonalcoholic juice spritzers: Pure white grape juice (or other fresh juices) and natural carbonated water with a twist.

Alcohol-free salty dog: Fresh-squeezed grapefruit juice with Celtic sea salt around the rim of the glass and a twist.

Virgin Mary: Fresh tomato juice, Tabasco sauce, and horseradish with a stick of celery.

Root-beer float: Pure, natural root beer, topped with vanilla rice-milk ice cream.

Healthy cappuccino: Raw chocolate, hemp-seed milk, reishi mushrooms, and stevia or agave.

❋❋❋ ❋❋❋

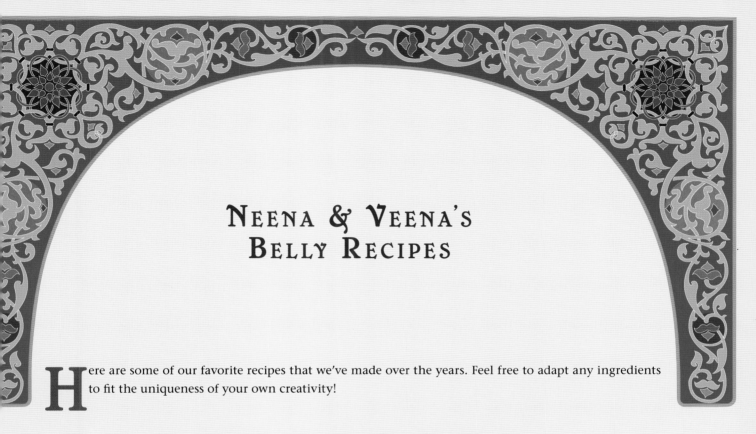

Neena & Veena's
Belly Recipes

Here are some of our favorite recipes that we've made over the years. Feel free to adapt any ingredients to fit the uniqueness of your own creativity!

Healthy Indian Kheer (Rice Pudding)

½ cup brown rice
4 cups soy, almond, or oat milk (for a thicker, creamier dish, use whole goat's milk)
¼ cup raw sugar
¼ cup unsalted, raw, chopped nuts (such as almonds, cashews, and/or pistachios)
Raisins or currants (optional)
1 teaspoon cardamom seeds
Pinch of saffron (optional)
½ teaspoon pure vanilla extract
1 teaspoon rosewater
Pinch of whole cloves
Pinch of cinnamon

Rinse the rice and soak for approximately 45 minutes; then drain and put in a heavy saucepan. Add milk to rice, boil, and immediately bring down to a simmer on low heat, cooking for approximately 1 to 1½ hours. Keep stirring and scraping the sides with a wooden spoon to prevent sticking and burning.

When it's thick and creamy, add sugar and stir for 3 minutes. Remove from heat and add fruit, nuts, cardamom seeds, cloves, and saffron; wait a few minutes and then add rosewater.

Although kheer can be served hot, we prefer it cold, with a sprinkle of cinnamon on top.

HEALTHY TABOULI

1 cup cracked wheat (bulgur) or quinoa (wheat-free)
1 cup boiling water
1 small organic tomato, chopped
1 small cucumber, peeled, chopped, and seeded
3 green onions, chopped
¼ finely chopped red onion (optional)
⅓ cup fresh chopped mint
1 cup fresh organic, chopped parsley
1 garlic clove, minced

Dressing:
¼ cup fresh organic lemon juice (remove seeds)
½ cup extra-virgin olive oil
¼ cup grape-seed oil (if you don't have grape-seed oil, you can use all olive oil)
1 teaspoon liquid aminos (optional)
Sea salt and pepper to taste

Soak the cracked wheat in the water for 20 minutes or until the water is absorbed (whichever comes first); if necessary after 20 minutes, drain and squeeze out any excess water. Combine the remaining ingredients in a medium bowl. Serve chilled or at room temperature.

Egyptian Tablich

1 large organic zucchini
Fresh organic green beans, cut
1 teaspoon (or to taste) curry powder
4 tablespoons olive oil
1 large yellow onion, chopped
1 small white onion, finely chopped
1 clove garlic, crushed
3 organic tomatoes, chopped
1 tablespoon tomato puree (unsweetened)
Fresh sage
Tarragon
Lemon peel
4 cups filtered water
2 cups organic brown rice
Liquid aminos to taste
Sea salt and fresh-ground pepper to taste

Cook rice in water, uncovered, until water boils out; drain if necessary. Add liquid aminos and stir. Separately, in a large skillet, sauté yellow onion and garlic clove in olive oil until translucent. Stir in tomatoes and cook until thickened; then stir in puree, salt, and pepper. Reduce heat and simmer for 10 minutes or until slightly thick. Add zucchini, green beans, and white onion; cook for approximately 10 minutes. Add the rest of the spices and simmer for 8 more minutes, then pour over rice.

EGG-WHITE OMELETTE

5–6 cage-free, hormone-free egg whites
½ teaspoon virgin coconut oil (or 1 tablespoon olive oil)

Veggies:
¾ cup chopped organic spinach
½ cup sliced zucchini
1 garlic clove, minced
¼ cup fresh mushrooms
¼ cup fresh red, yellow, and/or green bell peppers

Heat oil in nonstick pan over medium-low heat. Sauté all ingredients for approximately 2 minutes. Beat eggs until fluffy, and pour into pan; cook eggs lightly over low heat, pushing sides of cooked eggs inward toward the center of the pan. Flip carefully with a spatula when eggs appear done and cook lightly a minute or two longer. Serve with sliced organic tomatoes and garnish with parsley.

Note: For "Jordanian" style, brown ¼ to ⅓ pound of ground lamb until light brown with some pink color; drain fat, absorbing extra fat with a paper towel, if needed. Add ½ cup chopped onion; 1 garlic clove; and cumin powder, thyme, and turmeric to taste. Stuff into folded egg-white omelette, spoon a little tahini sauce over it (optional), and sprinkle a few chopped olives on top. Garnish with parsley.

BABA GHANOUSH (EGGPLANT DIP)

1 large organic eggplant
3 cloves of organic garlic, mashed into paste
4 tablespoons fresh organic lemon juice
4 tablespoons tahini (optional)
    Note: Turkish style is without tahini.
Sea salt
Red pepper
Olive oil
Fresh parsley, chopped

Place eggplant over the flame of a gas stove, turning it occasionally, and cook until the skin is blackened (our mom used to cook it in a hot oven). Put over the sink and pour cold water until it's cool enough to handle; then peel skin, and chop into small pieces. Add garlic and lemon juice and mash to a smooth consistency. Add tahini (optional). Spoon into a bowl, top with a little olive oil, red pepper, and chopped parsley.

FUL MADAMIS (FAVA BEANS)

2 cups dried fava beans (large or small size)
Filtered water for soaking
6 cups filtered water for cooking
1 large organic tomato, coarsely chopped (optional)
1 small organic yellow onion, finely chopped
4 garlic cloves, minced
1 teaspoon ground cumin
Sea salt
Freshly ground pepper
Pinch of red chili pepper
Juice of ½–1 organic lemon

Garnishes:
Fresh parsley (preferably Italian)
Chopped scallions
Organic lemon wedges
Extra-virgin olive oil
Hard-boiled eggs, chopped (optional)

Soak beans in a generous amount of filtered water in the refrigerator overnight, then drain. Put the water for cooking in a saucepan and add beans, making sure that they're covered by the water. Bring to a boil, reduce heat to low, and cover, simmering until beans are tender—approximately 1½ to 5 hours, depending on size of beans. When the beans are ready, add onions, tomato, garlic, cumin, salt, ground pepper, and chili pepper (to taste). Squeeze in the juice of ½ to 1 lemon and stir.

Spoon each serving into a separate bowl and mash beans slightly. Top with a little olive oil and parsley; serve other garnishes on side.

GREEN MOROCCAN MINT TEA

½ teaspoon pure green tea
Turbinado sugar to taste (or honey)
8–10 large fresh mint leaves
1 cup water
1 sprig of mint per glass to be served

Crush mint leaves in boiling water; add tea to water and let steep for 5 minutes. Put a small sprig of mint in thick, small juice glasses; strain tea into glasses; and serve sugar on the side.

CAIRO KABOBS

2 lbs. lamb loins
Juice of ½ organic lemon
1–2 tablespoons olive oil
Sea salt
Fresh-ground pepper
Bay leaves
Dash of turmeric powder
1 medium organic onion, sliced
3 medium organic tomatoes, sliced
Organic green and red bell pepper
Whole organic mushrooms
Organic garlic cloves

Mix olive oil, lemon juice, and spices; set aside. Trim the fat off the lamb, and cut meat into 1-inch cubes. Rub oil mixture into meat, and place in a dish. Cover with garlic cloves, mushrooms, tomatoes, onions, peppers, and a few bay leaves. Place in refrigerator for 4–5 hours or overnight. Arrange meat on skewers, alternating it with tomatoes, onions, mushrooms, and garlic. Cook over grill or in preheated broiler.

164

Dolmas

50 grape leaves
Sea salt
Juice of 2 organic lemons

Stuffing:
1 cup long-grain brown rice
1 medium organic onion, chopped
Olive oil
1 large organic tomato, chopped (optional)
2 tablespoons fresh parsley minced
2 tablespoons fresh mint leaves
2 teaspoons dill
¼ cup currants
¼ cup pine nuts or walnuts
Sea salt
Fresh-ground pepper

Place rice in a bowl with cold filtered water and let stand for 30 minutes. Put currants in a separate bowl, add hot water, and let stand for 20 to 30 minutes (until plump). At the same time, toast pine nuts in the oven for approximately 5 minutes.

Drain rice. In pan, sauté onions with spices in olive oil for 2–3 minutes. Add rice and sauté for another 2–3 minutes; set aside.

Soak fresh grape leaves in hot water for 15 minutes. Rinse in cool water, then squeeze out water and cut off stems. Line the bottom of a pot with a layer of grape leaves, shiny side down. Place 1 tablespoon of stuffing near the stem end of each leaf. Fold ends of leaf in and roll, but not too tight, as the rice needs room to expand. Arrange leaves in rows in the pot and sprinkle with salt.

Press leaves down with an inverted dish; then cover with water until it reaches the dish, and pour ¼ cup olive oil around the leaves. Cover pot and cook on the stove on low for about 1 hour or until tender. Remove from heat and add lemon juice on top. Serve cold or hot with side of lemon wedges.

Note: For non-vegetarians, add ½ to 1 pound of ground lamb to the stuffing.

REFRESHING YOGURT-MINT DRINK

2 cups goats' milk yogurt
1 cup water
15–20 fresh mint leaves
Cumin
Ice

Combine water and mint in a blender for 20 seconds. Add the rest of the ingredients and blend for an extra 20 seconds. Pour into glasses and add a garnish of mint leaves to each one. Serves 4–6.

You can substitute a pinch of sea salt for the mint; for Indian style, add cardamom; for a sweet lassi, add touch of raw sugar instead of sea salt. Yogurt drinks are a favorite in much of North Africa, Middle East, Pakistan, and India. In most of the Middle East they're called *laban;* in India, they're *lassi;* in Iran, they're *abdug;* and in Armenia, the name is *tahn.*

* * * * *

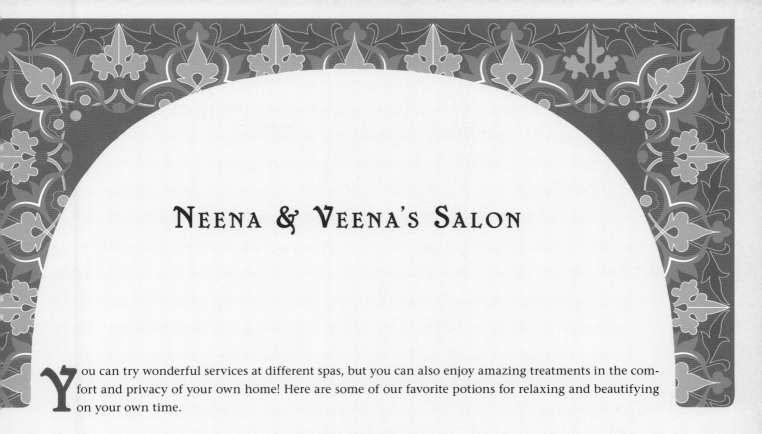

NEENA & VEENA'S SALON

Y ou can try wonderful services at different spas, but you can also enjoy amazing treatments in the comfort and privacy of your own home! Here are some of our favorite potions for relaxing and beautifying on your own time.

BEAUTIFUL BATHS

We offer an array of options from milk to mandarins, so pick your pleasure!

— **Egyptian milk bath:** To make your own milk bath, simply toss a packet of powdered milk under running bathwater or use a quart to a gallon of whole liquid milk. Don't worry: It's not fattening—and you don't have to worry about being lactose intolerant!

It might seem silly at first, but Cleopatra in her milk bath has a lot in common with the luxurious sensuality of belly dance. As you slide into your creamy, healing water, imagine you're in ancient Egypt, where even common women washed their faces in milk. And in India, bathing in fresh, whole milk has a long tradition as a beautifier and purifier. Hindus also bathe statues of their deities in this symbol of nourishment, as well as honey and oils.

So this bath might make you feel like a queen on the inside—and it will definitely make you look like one on the outside! Milk is loaded with lactic acid, which gently removes dead skin leaving you as soft as baby . . . or a goddess.

— **Dancer's muscle soother:** Veena and I swear by this soak. When we've been dancing a lot and feel sore—say, after a two-hour performance—we each take a warm bath and throw in 1 or 2 cups of sea or Epsom salt and 1 cup of apple-cider vinegar. After soaking for about 20 minutes, any soreness just dissolves away. This oceanic solution not only relaxes the muscles, it soothes the skin and helps it dispose of toxic wastes.

To just treat your feet, pour ⅓ cup each of salt and vinegar in a bowl of warm water big enough to soak your feet. This is almost as soothing as a massage!

— **Herbal tension tamer:** After a long day of taking care of business, I love taking a relaxing herbal bath. Chamomile has soothing, healing properties that ease away the stress. Simply brew 3 cups of very strong chamomile tea and add to your bathwater. One of our friends in Egypt loves to use elder or lime flowers, which are also very relaxing.

AROMATHERAPY BATHS

— **Tropical-citrus zinger:** Add about 1 cup of juice of any one or more citrus fruits (such as lemons, oranges, and grapefruits) to warm bathwater. The acid in the fruit kills bacteria, purifies the skin, balances excess oil, and brightens your mood. Sometimes I like to add about a cup of sea salt—then you've got Gatorade!

— **Yummy-vanilla thrilla:** Add ¼ cup of pure vanilla extract or whole vanilla bean to warm bathwater. This substance has the ability to lift spirits and is said to be one of the male sex's major turn-ons! (Juniper, mint, rosemary, and angelica are other stimulating herbs.)

— **Egyptian rose garden:** Add 10–12 drops of rose oil to warm bathwater. It hydrates skin, is a wonderful scent, and helps prevent spider veins. For the ultimate in luxury, also toss in a handful of fresh rose petals, available at flower shops.

— **Mediterranean-lavender soother:** Put 2 tablespoons of dried lavender and 1 tablespoon of fennel seeds in a piece of cheesecloth; knot closed firmly and submerge in the bathwater. You can also put a few drops of lavender oil directly in the bath. This is an ancient relaxing fragrance that will ease you gently into a restful night's sleep. Fennel is good for digestion and colds, and also has a soothing scent.

— **Pine-forest interlude:** Place a handful of pine needles in a square of cheesecloth; knot closed firmly. Toss this into a warm bath, and you'll be transported to a calming, secluded pine forest.

— **Bubble bath:** This isn't just for children! Take your favorite scented bubble bath, which you can combine with any of the other above ingredients. The luxurious sensuality of the foam will help you kiss your tension good-bye . . . and you can always invite that special someone to join you. . . .

SENSUAL SCRUBS

Veena and I sometimes make our own scrubs. It's a fun way to get a lot of variety in the bath and shower, without spending a lot of money! Give these recipes a try and you'll see what I mean. . . .

— **Basic scrub:** For an easy exfoliant, my sister and I just combine ½ cup sea salt; ½ cup almond, apricot-kernel, avocado, or another light oil; 1 tablespoon cosmetic-grade vitamin E oil; and 20 drops of an essential oil such as lavender. An even simpler recipe is to mix almond oil with Celtic sea salt, adding a few drops of essential oils if you like.

— **Golden Ayurvedic scrub:** In India, it's traditional to use chickpea flour combined with herbs and spices to give your skin a thorough cleaning. The soft powder has just the right amount of abrasiveness for gentle exfoliation, so you can use it every day. Simply combine 4 tablespoons of chickpea flour and 1 teaspoon of turmeric. Add enough liquid—preferably milk, but you can use water—to form a paste. Use this in the tub before you run the shower, and be careful, because the turmeric can stain towels. (Be sure to rinse well to remove any residue.) Not only does this concoction kill bacteria, but it also gives you a lovely golden glow and leaves your skin silky smooth and soft.

— **Freshening-oatmeal scrub:** Mix together 3 cups traditional, old-fashioned, uncooked oatmeal; 2 cups wheat bran; and ¼ cup aloe-vera gel. If you like, you can add a hint of Indian-inspired tamarind for an exotic scent. Spoon the mixture into a piece of fine-mesh cheesecloth or a nylon "knee-high," and add the package to your bathwater. After soaking, rub the bag over your body to cleanse, smooth, and freshen your skin. (In a pinch, you can just use the oatmeal.)

Must-Have Masks

— **Moisturizing-banana mask:** Mash together 1 very ripe banana; 1 teaspoon almond, apricot, sesame, or olive oil; and 1 drop orange essential oil. Apply to your face and leave on for 15–20 minutes.

— **Heavenly honey-banana mask:** Mash together 1 very ripe banana and one tablespoon honey. Apply to your face and leave for 15–20 minutes, then rinse.

— **Oil and acne-taming apple mask:** Mix together 1 grated apple and 5 tablespoons of honey. Apply to your face and leave for 10 minutes, then rinse. (A mashed-up, ripe tomato can also work to control excess oil, and melon juice is effective for summertime flare-ups.)

— **Papaya glow:** Mix together 1 tablespoon each of fuller's earth, honey, and mashed papaya. Apply to your face and leave on for 20 minutes

— **Yogurt pick-me-up:** Combine 1 teaspoon plain yogurt with the juice of ¼ orange. Smooth onto your face and leave on for 5 minutes. You'll feel pleasantly revived!

— **Rosy rejuvenator:** Grind a handful of organic rose petals into a paste; apply to clean skin and leave on for 15–25 minutes. Then rinse for a smooth and rosy complexion. In India and the Middle East, rosewater is a major beauty product, as well as an ingredient in many recipes. We think it's a wonderful way to wash your face. To make your own, boil fresh rose petals (make sure they're organic!) and use this liquid instead of plain water as a final rinse for your face.

Pampering Hand and Foot Treatments

— **Mini-milk bath for hands:** Soak your hands for 5 minutes in milk to strengthen the nails and hydrate the skin.

— **Honey moisturizing mask for hands:** Wash hands thoroughly with warm water; then, using a coarse washcloth, rub them briskly. While skin is still slightly damp, apply a mixture of one teaspoon honey and one teaspoon olive oil. Place hands in small plastic bags or gloves, and then in a pair of cotton gloves, for 30 minutes. The trapped body heat helps the treatment penetrate.

— **Eastern spicy soak for feet:** Combine 1 cup of fresh lemon juice, a sprinkle of ground cinnamon (or a stick of this spice), flower petals such as roses or jasmine (optional), 1 tablespoon of almond oil, and ¼ cup of milk. Pour this in a basin or bowl big enough to soak your feet in. Add enough water to cover your feet (cool in summer, warm in winter) and soak for about 15 minutes. This combination leaves skin refreshed and smelling sweet.

— **Foot scrub:** After soaking feet in warm water for at least 10 minutes, use a foot scrub to exfoliate any dead skin cells (try one of our body scrubs!). This reveals a new, smooth layer of clean skin on your feet and lower legs. If you have stubborn corns or calluses, we recommend over-the-counter remedies from the drugstore, but you may need to have them professionally removed. In Islamic hammams, decallusing was an important treatment because it allowed fatigue and bad vapors to flow down and out of the body through the soles of the feet.

— **Minty-fresh massage:** You can't massage your whole body yourself, but you can work on your hands and feet. Combine 3 tablespoons grape-seed oil, 3 drops eucalyptus oil, 4–5 drops rosemary oil, and 2–3 drops peppermint oil; pour the solution into a small bottle and seal well. Warm up the oil before massaging your hands or feet. For extra softness, wear socks to bed after your massage. You'll wake up with soft, smooth, minty feet!

* * * * * *

ABOUT THE AUTHORS

Neena & Veena, aka "the Bellytwins," are a fascinating and powerful blend of East and West and inner and outer beauty. Born and raised in Northern California, they're proof that you can be smart, sexy, spiritual, healthy, *and* have a successful and satisfying life. They show how their own obstacles—including growing up poor and having an ill mother—actually helped them express their true selves and live more fulfilling, positive lives. They've traveled throughout the Middle East and India to develop their techniques, and have performed worldwide for numerous top celebrities.

From their home base in Los Angeles, Neena & Veena have taught many people, including Hollywood's elite, how to shimmy their way to better bodies and better health. As artists, they've performed on hundreds of stages; appeared in films, TV programs, and music videos, including the American Music Awards and the Academy Awards; and have been featured in countless magazines, including *Vogue* and *In Style.* They also have 12 extremely popular workout and dance DVDs and videos—*they've sold millions!*—which are available in major retail stores and online, with more products to come. Through their Website, **www.bellytwins.com,** Neena & Veena can stay in touch with a whole new world of ardent fans.

Nancy Bruning has authored or co-authored more than 20 books, most of them about health, alternative therapies, spirituality, and beauty. Her most recent works are: *Dare to Lose: 4 Simple Steps to a Better Body* and *Rhythms and Cycles: Sacred Patterns in Everyday Life.* She's written two books about Ayurveda, the health system from India: *Ayurveda: The A–Z Guide to Healing Techniques from Ancient India* and *Effortless Beauty.* She's also written books about vitamin and mineral supplementation, menopause, breast implants, cancer chemotherapy, swimming, childhood asthma, homeopathy, and more. An avid fan and student of belly dance, Nancy is also a certified personal trainer and massage practitioner. She recently relocated from California to New York City.

✳ ✳ ✳   ✳ ✳ ✳

Hay House Titles of Related Interest

BODYCHANGE™ : *The 21-Day Fitness Program for Changing Your Body . . . and Changing Your Life,* by Montel Williams and Wini Linguvic

THE BODY CHALLENGE SUCCESS PROGRAM FOR THE WHOLE FAMILY, by Pamela Peeke, MD, MPH, FACP

FRANK SEPE'S ABS-OLUTELY PERFECT PLAN FOR A FLATTER STOMACH: *The Only Abs Book You'll Ever Need*

GETTING IN THE GAP: *Making Conscious Contact with God Through Meditation,* by Dr. Wayne W. Dyer (book-with-CD)

THE NATURAL NUTRITION NO-COOK BOOK: *Delicious Food for YOU . . . and Your PETS!,* by Kymythy Schultze

THE RIGHT WEIGH: *Six Steps to Permanent Weight Loss Used by More Than 100,000 People,* by Rena Greenberg

SHAPE® MAGAZINE'S ULTIMATE BODY BOOK: *4 Weeks to Your Best Abs, Butt, Thighs, and More!,* by Linda Shelton, with Angela Hynes

SIMPLY WOMAN: *The 12-Week Body-Mind-Soul Total Transformation Program,* by Crystal Andrus (includes a DVD)

THE TRUTH: *The Only Fitness Book You'll Ever Need,* by Frank Sepe

ULTIMATE PILATES: *Achieve the Perfect Body Shape,* by Dreas Reyneke

YOGA PURE AND SIMPLE: *Transform Your Body Shape with the Program That Really Works,* by Kisen

We hope you enjoyed this Hay House book. If you'd like to receive a free catalog featuring additional Hay House books and products, or if you'd like information about the Hay Foundation, please contact:

Hay House, Inc.
P.O. Box 5100
Carlsbad, CA 92018-5100

(760) 431-7695 or **(800) 654-5126**
(760) 431-6948 (fax) or **(800) 650-5115 (fax)**
www.hayhouse.com

✳ ✳ ✳

Published and distributed in Australia by:
Hay House Australia Pty. Ltd. • 18/36 Ralph St. • Alexandria NSW 2015
Phone: 612-9669-4299 • *Fax:* 612-9669-4144 • www.hayhouse.com.au

Published and distributed in the United Kingdom by:
Hay House UK, Ltd. • Unit 62, Canalot Studios •
222 Kensal Rd., London W10 5BN • *Phone:* 44-20-8962-1230
Fax: 44-20-8962-1239 • www.hayhouse.co.uk

Published and distributed in the Republic of South Africa by:
Hay House SA (Pty), Ltd., P.O. Box 990, Witkoppen 2068
Phone/Fax: 27-11-706-6612 • orders@psdprom.co.za

Distributed in Canada by:
Raincoast • 9050 Shaughnessy St., Vancouver, B.C. V6P 6E5
Phone: (604) 323-7100 • *Fax:* (604) 323-2600

✳ ✳ ✳

Tune in to **www.hayhouseradio.com**™ for the best in inspirational talk radio featuring top Hay House authors! And, sign up via the Hay House USA Website to receive the Hay House online newsletter and stay informed about what's going on with your favorite authors. You'll receive bimonthly announcements about: Discounts and Offers, Special Events, Product Highlights, Free Excerpts, Giveaways, and more!
www.hayhouse.com